Kids' Lunches
Eat In - Take Out

www.companyscoming.com
visit our website

Front Cover

1. Salmon Cups, page 46
2. Cinnamon Straws, page 21
3. Hero Sandwich, page 117
4. Chocolate Chip Granola Bars, page 26
5. Blueberry Pineapple Cooler, page 20
6. Peas 'N' Pasta Salad, page 103
7. Honey Mustard Dunk, page 32

Back Cover

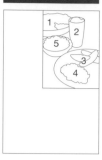

1. Spicy Taco Pie, page 50
2. Lemon Cola Float, page 20
3. Nacho Skins, page 43
4. Creamy Macaroni & Cheese, page 64
5. Bean & Tomato Salad, page 100

Kids' Lunches

First Printing August 2012

Library and Archives Canada Cataloguing in Publication

Paré, Jean, date
Kids' lunches : eat in, take out / Jean Paré.
(Original series)
Includes index.
At head of title: Company's Coming.
ISBN 978-1-897477-87-8
1. Lunchbox cooking. 2. Cookbooks. I. Title.
II. Series: Paré, Jean, 1927- . Original series.
TX735.P375 2012   641.5'3   C2012-900709-9

Published by
Company's Coming Publishing Limited
2311 – 96 Street
Edmonton, Alberta, Canada T6N 1G3
Tel: 780-450-6223 Fax: 780-450-1857
www.companyscoming.com

Company's Coming is a registered trademark owned by Company's Coming Publishing Limited

We acknowledge the financial support of the Government of Canada through the Canada Book Fund for our publishing activities.

Printed in China

We gratefully acknowledge the following suppliers for their generous support of our Test and Photography Kitchens:

Broil King Barbecues
Corelle®
Hamilton Beach® Canada
Lagostina®
Proctor Silex® Canada
Tupperware®

Our special thanks to the following business for providing props for photography:

Creations by Design
Edmonton Wedding & Party Centre
La Cache
Le Gnome
Mystique Pottery & Gifts
Stokes
The Basket House
The Bay

Kids' Cookbook Collections

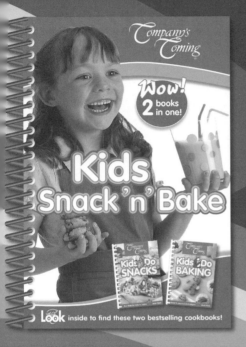

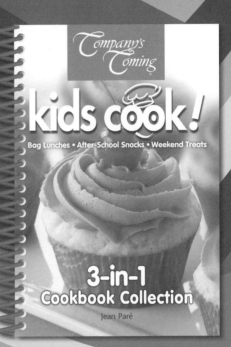

Fun Food for Kids!

Company's Coming Cookbooks

Quick & easy recipes; everyday ingredients!

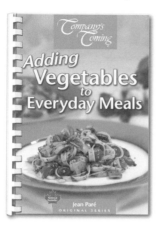

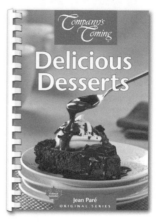

Original Series

- Softcover, 160 pages
- 126 all-new recipes
- Lay-flat plastic comb binding
- Nutrition information

Original Series

- Softcover, 160 pages
- 135 all-new recipes
- Lay-flat plastic comb binding
- Nutrition information

Original Series

- Softcover, 160 pages
- 135 all-new recipes
- Lay-flat plastic comb binding
- Nutrition information

Original Series

- Softcover, 160 pages
- 127 all-new recipes
- Lay-flat plastic comb binding
- Nutrition information

For a complete listing of our cookbooks, visit our website:
www.companyscoming.com

Table of Contents

A note to parents

This book is intended for your children to use. It has been especially written for kids aged 8 to 15 years. Please supervise them when necessary. The handling of sharp knives, boiling liquids, and hot pans needs to be monitored carefully with younger children.

The Company's Coming Story

Jean Paré (pronounced "jeen PAIR-ee") grew up understanding that the combination of family, friends and home cooking is the best recipe for a good life. From her mother, she learned to appreciate good cooking, while her father praised even her earliest attempts in the kitchen. When Jean left home, she took with her a love of cooking, many family recipes and an intriguing desire to read cookbooks as if they were novels!

"Never share a recipe you wouldn't use yourself."

When her four children had all reached school age, Jean volunteered to cater the 50th anniversary celebration of the Vermilion School of Agriculture, now Lakeland College, in Alberta, Canada. Working out of her home, Jean prepared a dinner for more than 1,000 people, launching a flourishing catering operation that continued for over 18 years. During that time, she had countless opportunities to test new ideas with immediate feedback—resulting in empty plates and contented customers! Whether preparing cocktail sandwiches for a house party or serving a hot meal for 1,500 people, Jean Paré earned a reputation for great food, courteous service and reasonable prices.

As requests for her recipes increased, Jean was often asked the question, "Why don't you write a cookbook?" Jean responded by teaming up with her son, Grant Lovig, in the fall of 1980 to form Company's Coming Publishing Limited. The publication of *150 Delicious Squares* on April 14, 1981 marked the debut of what would soon become one of the world's most popular cookbook series.

The company has grown since those early days when Jean worked from a spare bedroom in her home. Nowadays every Company's Coming recipe is *kitchen-tested* before it is approved for publication.

Company's Coming cookbooks are distributed in Canada, the United States, Australia and other world markets. Bestsellers many times over in English, Company's Coming cookbooks have also been published in French and Spanish.

Familiar and trusted in home kitchens around the world, Company's Coming cookbooks are offered in a variety of formats. Highly regarded as kitchen workbooks, the softcover Original Series, with its lay-flat plastic comb binding, is still a favourite among readers.

Jean Paré's approach to cooking has always called for *quick and easy recipes* using *everyday ingredients*. That view has served her well. The recipient of many awards, including the Queen Elizabeth Golden Jubilee Medal, Jean was appointed Member of the Order of Canada, her country's highest lifetime achievement honour.

Jean continues to share what she calls The Golden Rule of Cooking: *Never share a recipe you wouldn't use yourself.* It's an approach that has worked—*millions of times over!*

Foreword

Time for lunch? Kids know the value of a good meal, and *Kids' Lunches* helps kids to prepare their own lunches. With a variety of lunch recipes that can be prepared and enjoyed at home or packed up and taken to school, your kids will now be able to relieve you of the task of preparing their midday meals—all while learning handy kitchen skills!

Find a wide range of recipes for soups, salads, desserts, pizzas, sandwiches and salads in this handy title. Hamburger Soup is always a classic, and this recipe can easily be doubled for a weekend lunch that the whole family can share. Pickly Pita Pockets can be made in advance and stored in the refrigerator for an easy on-the-go lunch that can be taken to the park, to school, or on a class field trip. Every kid knows that no lunch is complete without dessert, so wrap things up with a few Chocolate Bar Cookies and a Strawberry Banana Slushy to wash them down. Kids can make use of our convenient home and bag lunch menu suggestions to put together perfect lunch pairings depending upon the day's plans.

Parents should always take the time to review our kitchen safety information with their kids before allowing them to start cooking, and parents should stay nearby in case our young chefs run into any obstacles while building their skills and confidence in the kitchen. Once your kids have decided upon a recipe, read through the entire recipe with them before they start cooking. This way you can help to prepare them for any challenges that they may encounter.

As your kids start to collect their ingredients, have them collect all the kitchen utensils and equipment listed in the "Get It Together" section of each recipe too—this way they won't be searching for tools at the last minute. A helpful utensil guide and glossary help kids to identify kitchen tools and learn common kitchen terms.

Kids learn so much from working in the kitchen—skills that they can build upon for the rest of their lives. Once you've covered the safety concerns with your kids, there's only one thing left to do: get ready, set, cook!

Jean Paré

Bossy Safety Stuff

I know, I know, you hate being told what to do, but here's why you should listen:

- Make sure the adults are OK with you cooking. And it helps to check if you can use up ingredients. (If you use up the cheese, how is Mom supposed to make her famous liver soup for supper?)

- Tie up long hair. It's gross to find a strand around the pasta, and it's worse to have it catch in a blender or singe on a burner.

- Same goes for loose clothing (well, you might not find it in the pasta). But tuck in those shirts and roll up those sleeves.

- Wash your hands with soap at the start, and every time you change ingredients. Grey cookie dough? Yuck! Onion-flavoured grey cookie dough? Double yuck!

- Dry your hands before plugging in appliances or touching sockets, otherwise you'll have an electrifying experience.

- Use oven mitts whenever you handle hot dishes or pans.

- Turn saucepan and frying pan handles toward the centre or the back of the stove so people can't knock them off the stove.

- Turn off the stove and oven when you're done.

- Be careful with hot water. Don't overfill a pan, and if it's too heavy for you to lift, please ask a grown-up for help.

- Wipe up spills, especially greasy ones, as soon as possible to prevent an indoor skating rink. Hot, soapy water will do the trick.

- If younger brothers and sisters are "helping," keep them away from sharp knives and hot stoves.

Basic Cooking Stuff

- Wash your hands before you start (see Bossy Safety Stuff, page 8).
- Read the recipe all the way through before you start.
- Gather your ingredients and equipment first. This prevents you from scrambling for a pancake lifter while the burger is burning.
- Wash your fruit and vegetables before cooking or eating.
- Use the size of pot/pan/plate, etc. that it says in the recipe. We've tested the recipes this way to make sure you'll succeed.
- Use the right measuring tools. See pages 12 to 13 for instructions.
- Do one recipe step at a time. The numbers beside our ingredients match the steps to keep you on track. Don't skip steps.
- As you finish with bowls and pans, pop them in the dishwasher or rinse them out. This prevents a humongous mess at the end.
- Did we mention a mess? Clean up when you're done, or you may be banned from the kitchen (except to wash everyone else's dishes)!

Ingredient Stuff

Say you're all ready to make the Hawaiian Grilled Cheese, and you discover there are no process cheese slices in the fridge. If your parents let you cut your Cheddar cheese block, you're all set to go. Just remember to cut thin slices, and have enough to cover the palm of an adult's hand.

The same goes for chocolate milk. You can make your own with regular milk and chocolate powder or syrup.

Don't substitute just anything, though. Ask an adult if you're thinking about using another ingredient for one that's listed in a recipe.

Glossary

Bake: To cook in an oven preheated to the temperature it says in the recipe. Use either the bottom rack or centre rack.

Batter: A mixture of flour, liquid and other ingredients that can be thin (such as pancake batter) or thick (such as muffin batter).

Beat: To mix two or more ingredients with a spoon, fork or electric mixer, using a circular motion.

Blend: To mix two or more ingredients together with a spoon, fork, electric mixer or electric blender until combined.

Boil: To heat a liquid in a saucepan until bubbles rise in a steady pattern and break on the surface. Steam also starts to rise from the surface.

Break an Egg: Tap the side of an egg on the edge of a bowl or cup to crack the shell. Place the tips of both thumbs in the crack and open the shell, letting the egg yolk and egg white drop into the bowl.

Broil: To cook under the top heating element in the oven. Use either the top rack or the upper rack.

Chill: To refrigerate until cold.

Chop: To cut food carefully into small pieces with a sharp knife on a cutting board; to chop finely is to cut foods as small as you can.

Combine: To put two or more ingredients together.

Cream: To beat an ingredient or combination of ingredients until the mixture is soft, smooth and "creamy."

Cut In: To combine solid fat (such as butter or margarine) with dry ingredients (such as flour) using a fork or pastry blender until the mixture looks like big crumbs the size of green peas.

Dice: To cut food into small 1/4 inch (6 mm) cube-shaped pieces.

Dip (into): To lower into a liquid either part way or all the way.

Drain: To strain away an unwanted liquid (such as water, fruit juice or grease) using a colander or strainer. Drain water or juice over the kitchen sink or in a bowl. Drain grease into a metal can, refrigerate, then throw away in the garbage after it hardens.

Drizzle: To dribble drops or lines of glaze or icing over food in a random manner from tines of a fork or the end of a spoon.

Fold: To mix gently, using a rubber spatula, by cutting down in the centre and lifting towards the edge of the bowl. Use a "down, up, over" movement, turning the bowl as you repeat.

Garnish: To decorate food with edible condiments such as parsley sprigs, fruit slices or vegetable cut-outs.

Heat: To make something warm or hot by placing the saucepan on the stove burner that is turned on to the level it says in the recipe.

Knead: To work dough into a smooth putty-like mass by folding and pressing using the heels of your hands.

Let Stand: To let a baked product cool slightly on a wire rack or hot pad, while still in its baking pan.

Mash: To squash cooked or very ripe foods with a fork or potato masher.

Melt: To heat a solid food such as butter, margarine, cheese or chocolate, until it turns into a liquid. Be careful not to burn it.

Mix (see **Combine**)

Mixing Just Until Moistened: To stir dry ingredients with liquid ingredients until dry ingredients are just wet. Mixture will still be lumpy.

Process: To mix or cut up food in a blender (or food processor) until it is the way it says in the recipe.

Sauté: To cook food quickly in a small amount of oil in a frying pan, wok or special sauté pan over medium heat.

Scramble-fry: To brown ground meat in hot oil using a spoon, fork or pancake lifter to break up the meat into small crumb-like pieces as it cooks.

Scrape: To use a rubber spatula to remove as much of a mixture as possible from inside a bowl or saucepan.

Separate an Egg (see **Break an Egg**)**:** Once the shell is open, carefully keep the egg yolk in one half shell and let the egg white drip into a small bowl or cup. Carefully pour the yolk into the other half shell, again letting any egg white drip into the bowl or cup. Be careful that the yolk does not break. Continue until there is no more egg white, except In the bowl or cup.

Simmer: To cook liquids in a saucepan over a low heat on the stove burner so that slow bubbles appear on the surface around the sides of the liquid.

Slice: To cut foods such as apples, carrots, tomatoes, meat or bread into thin sections or pieces, using a sharp knife.

Spoon (into): To move ingredients from one container to another, using a spoon to scoop from one and drop into the other.

Spread: To cover the surface of one product (generally a more solid food) with another product (generally a softer food such as icing or butter).

Stir: To mix two or more ingredients with a spoon, using a circular motion.

Toast: To brown lightly in a toaster or frying pan or under the broiler in the oven.

Toss: To mix salad ingredients lightly with a lifting motion, using two forks, two spoons or salad tongs.

Equipment & Utensils

Baking sheet

Bread knife

Broiler pan

Casserole dish

Colander

Blender

Cookie sheet

Cutting board

Dry measures

Electric frying pan

Electric mixer

Frying pan

Hot pad

Loaf pan

Ice-cream scoop

Grater

Liquid measures

Measuring spoons

Microwave oven

Mixing bowls

Mixing spoons (long-handled)

Muffin pan

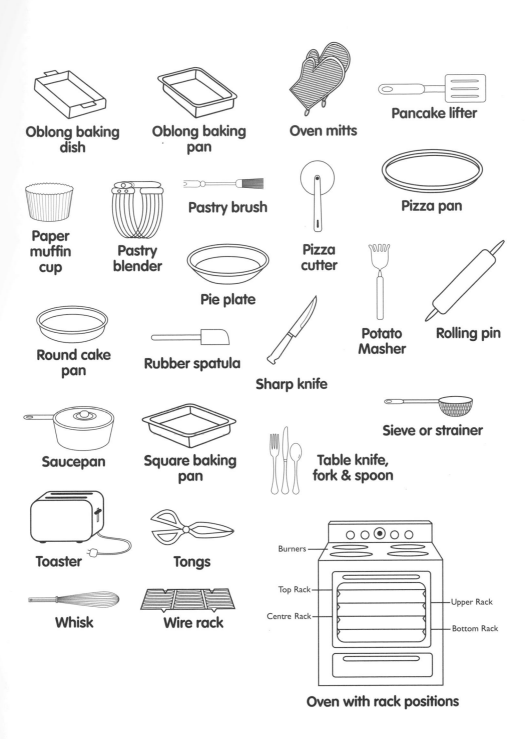

Oblong baking dish

Oblong baking pan

Oven mitts

Pancake lifter

Paper muffin cup

Pastry blender

Pastry brush

Pizza cutter

Pizza pan

Pie plate

Round cake pan

Rubber spatula

Sharp knife

Potato Masher

Rolling pin

Saucepan

Square baking pan

Table knife, fork & spoon

Sieve or strainer

Toaster

Tongs

Burners

Top Rack

Centre Rack

Upper Rack

Bottom Rack

Whisk

Wire rack

Oven with rack positions

Menu Suggestions

Home Lunch #1
Chicken Thumbs, page 42
Dilly Pickle Dip, page 32
Potato Salad, page 96
Easy Raisin Cookies, page 25
Melon Milkshake, page 19

Home Lunch #2
Loaded Quesadilla, page 73
Peas 'N' Pasta Salad, page 103
Applesauce Jellied Dessert, page 25
Strawberry Banana Slushy, page 16

Home Lunch #3
Nacho Skins, page 43
Corn Chowder, page 134
Hot Tortilla Dip, page 31 (with
    vegetables and tortilla chips)

Home Lunch #4
Build-Your-Pita Pizzas, page 85
Colour-Full Bean Soup, page 137
Sour Cream & Onion Dip, page 39
    (with vegetables)
Lemon Cola Float, page 20

Home Lunch #5
Creamy Beef 'N' Pasta, page 61
Cottage Cheese Salad, page 101
Apricot Logs, page 26
Eggnog, page 15

Home Lunch #6
Creamy Macaroni & Cheese, page 64
Tomato & Mozza Salad, page 99
S'Mores Squares, page 27
Strawberry Pineapple Cooler, page 20

Home Lunch #7
Quick Bread "Sandwich," page 55
Hamburger Soup, page 135
Garlic Cheese Dip, page 33
    (with vegetables)
Snap Gingers, page 29

Bag Lunch #1
Salmon Cups, page 46
Seeded Cheese, page 44
Rice Salad, page 98
Apple-Crisp Cookies, page 30

Bag Lunch #2
Veggie Bagel, page 121
Cucumber & Pea Salad, page 98
Chocolate Chip Granola Bars, page 26
Raspberry Pineapple Cooler, page 20

Bag Lunch #3
Individual Stuffed Pizzas, page 86
Marinated Vegetables, page 97
Cinnamon Straws, page 21
Blueberry Pineapple Cooler, page 20

Bag Lunch #4
Hero Sandwich, page 117
Tortellini Salad, page 95
Garlic Mustard Dip, page 33
    (with vegetables)
Chocolate Bar Cookies, page 23

Bag Lunch #5
Barbecue Beef Buns, page 112
Bean & Tomato Salad, page 100
Bolts 'N' Things, page 127

Bag Lunch #6
Ham & Cheese Delights, page 145
Peanut Butter Pudding Dip, page 38
    (with fresh fruit)
Fruity Granola, page 128
Veggie Cooler, page 15

Bag Lunch #7
Vegetable Roll, page 140
Ham & Melon Kabobs, page 44
Pepper-Corn Crackers, page 48
Spicy Corn Corn, page 130

Veggie Cooler

A delicious way to get your vegetables. Smooth and refreshing.

Get It Together: liquid measures, dry measures, blender

1.			
Tomato juice	1 1/2 cups	375 mL
Chopped celery	1/2 cup	125 mL
Chopped cucumber	1/2 cup	125 mL
Grated carrot	1/2 cup	125 mL
Hot pepper sauce, dash (optional)		

1. Put all 5 ingredients into the blender. Process until smooth. Cover. Chill in the refrigerator for several hours or overnight. Makes 2 1/3 cups (575 mL).

Pictured on page 17.

Eggnog

A perfect homemade version for the younger set.

Get It Together: measuring spoons, blender, liquid measures, ice-cream scoop

1. Large egg (see Note)	1	1
Granulated sugar	1 tbsp.	15 mL
2. Vanilla flavouring	1/2 tsp.	2 mL
Salt, sprinkle		
Milk	1/2 cup	125 mL
Ground nutmeg	1/8 tsp.	0.5 mL
3. Scoops of vanilla ice cream	2	2

1. Put the egg and sugar into the blender. Process until thick and lemon coloured.

2. Add the next 4 ingredients. Process.

3. Add the ice cream. Process until smooth. Serve immediately. Makes 1 cup (250 mL).

Note: Keep the egg in the refrigerator until you are ready to use it.

Pictured on page 18.

Strawberry Banana Slushy

A thick, rich shake.

Get It Together: dry measures, measuring spoons, liquid measures, blender

1.	**Lemon, vanilla or strawberry yogurt**	3/4 cup	175 mL
	Skim milk powder	2 tbsp.	30 mL
	Banana	1	1
	Milk	1 cup	250 mL
2.	**Large frozen strawberries**	5	5

1. Put the yogurt, milk powder, banana and milk into the blender. Process until smooth.

2. While the blender is processing, add the strawberries, 1 at a time, through the opening in the lid. Process until smooth and creamy. Makes 3 1/2 cups (875 mL).

1. Veggie Cooler, page 15
2. Crunchy Potato Salad, page 102
3. Tuna Buns, page 111
4. Easy Raisin Cookies, page 25
5. Hot Tortilla Dip, page 31

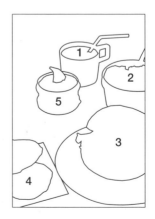

Melon Milkshake

Very refreshing.

Get It Together: table spoon, small bowl, liquid measures, measuring spoons, blender

1. **Cantaloupe (or honeydew melon), see Note**	1/2	1/2
2. **Milk**	1 1/2 cups	375 mL
Liquid honey	1 tbsp.	15 mL

1. Remove the seeds of the melon with the spoon. Scoop the melon out of the skin into the bowl. Freeze for 1 hour until solid. Cover with plastic wrap if freezing longer.

2. Put the milk and honey into the blender. Add the frozen melon. Process until smooth. Drink immediately. Makes about 4 cups (1 L).

Note: The amount of the drink will depend on the size of the cantaloupe or melon.

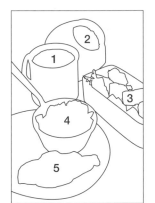

1. Eggnog, page 15
2. Fruity Granola, page 128
3. Ham & Melon Kabobs, page 44
4. Tortellini Salad, page 95
5. Ham & Cheese Delights, page 145

Strawberry Pineapple Cooler

A lovely pink colour with light pink foam on top. The soft drink adds a little fizz.

Get It Together: liquid measures, measuring spoons, blender, mixing spoon

1. Pineapple juice, chilled   1 cup   250 mL
   Skim milk powder   2 tbsp.   30 mL
   Large frozen strawberries   3   3

2. Ginger ale (or club soda), optional   1/2 cup   125 mL

1. Combine the pineapple juice and milk powder in the blender. Cover and process for 10 seconds. While the blender is processing, add the strawberries, 1 at a time, through the opening in the lid. Process until smooth.

2. Stir in the ginger ale if you wish to have a fizzy cooler. Makes 1 1/3 cups (325 mL).

RASPBERRY PINEAPPLE COOLER: Follow the directions for the Strawberry Pineapple Cooler, substituting 1/2 cup (125 mL) of raspberries for the strawberries.

BLUEBERRY PINEAPPLE COOLER: Follow the directions for the Strawberry Pineapple Cooler, substituting 1/2 cup (125 mL) of blueberries for the strawberries.

Pictured on the front cover.

Lemon Cola Float

The perfect beverage to have at home as a treat for lunch.

Get It Together: liquid measures, tall glass, ice-cream scoop

1. Cola soft drink, chilled   1 cup   250 mL
   Scoops of lemon sherbet   2   2

1. Pour the soft drink into the glass. Add the lemon sherbet. Makes 1 float.

Pictured on page 53 and on back cover.

Cinnamon Straws

Try these dipped in Applesauce, page 22. They freeze well.

Get It Together: medium bowl, measuring spoons, table fork, rolling pin, ruler, table knife, small cup, mixing spoon, cutting board, sharp knife, baking sheet, oven mitts, wire rack

1. **Envelope of pie crust mix**	1 x 9 1/2 oz.	1 x 270 g
Cold water	6 tbsp.	100 mL
All-purpose flour, as needed, to prevent sticking while rolling		
2. **Tub margarine, divided**	2 tbsp.	30 mL
Brown sugar, packed	2 tbsp.	30 mL
Ground cinnamon	1 tbsp.	15 mL

1. Place the oven rack in the centre position. Turn the oven on to 400°F (200°C). Place the pie crust mix in the bowl. Add the cold water, 1 tbsp. (15 mL) at a time, stirring with the fork after each addition. Form the dough into a ball. Divide the dough in half. Sprinkle some flour on the working surface. Roll out 1/2 of the dough into a 5 x 11 inch (12.5 x 28 cm) rectangle, about 1/8 inch (3 mm) thick.

2. Spread 1 tbsp. (15 mL) of the margarine over 1/2 of the rectangle, right to the edges. Combine the sugar and cinnamon in the small cup. Sprinkle 1/2 of the sugar mixture over the margarine. Fold the uncovered pastry half over the cinnamon half. Gently roll into a 5 x 11 inch (12.5 x 28 cm) rectangle, 1/8 inch (3 mm) thick. Set on the cutting board. Use the sharp knife to cut strips across the dough, each strip about 1/2 inch (12 mm) wide. Twist each strip 2 to 3 times and lay them on the ungreased baking sheet. Repeat with the second 1/2 of the dough. Bake in the oven for about 11 minutes until crisp and lightly browned. Use the oven mitts to remove the baking sheet to the wire rack. Makes 44 to 48 straws.

Pictured on the front cover.

Applesauce

Great by itself, or use it in other recipes.

Get It Together: cutting board, sharp knife, medium microwave-safe bowl, measuring spoons, plastic wrap, microwave oven, oven mitts, hot pad, mixing spoon, potato masher (or table fork)

1.
Large apples, peeled	3	3
Brown sugar, packed	1 tbsp.	15 mL
Ground cinnamon, sprinkle		

1. Using the cutting board, slice the apple off of the core in fairly large pieces, approximately 8. Discard the core. Put the slices into the bowl. Sprinkle with the sugar and cinnamon. Cover the bowl with plastic wrap. Microwave on high (100%) for 5 minutes. Using the oven mitts, remove the bowl from the oven to the hot pad. Slowly fold back the plastic wrap, being very careful not to burn yourself as the hot steam escapes. Stir. Cover the bowl again and microwave on high (100%) for 5 minutes. Using the oven mitts, remove the bowl to the hot pad. Let the mixture stand for 15 minutes to cool. Mash the cooled mixture with the potato masher until it is a chunky consistency. Makes 1 2/3 cups (400 mL).

Yummy Oatmeal Bars

Sweet and crunchy. Cuts well. Dough is very stiff but everything will mix in eventually.

Get It Together: 9 x 9 inch (23 x 23 cm) square baking pan, liquid measures, dry measures, large microwave-safe bowl, mixing spoon, microwave oven

1.
Liquid honey	2/3 cup	150 mL
Peanut butter	1/2 cup	125 mL
Butterscotch chips	3/4 cup	175 mL
Large marshmallows	10	10

2.
Quick-cooking rolled oats (not instant)	2 cups	500 mL
Sunflower seeds	1/4 cup	60 mL
Crisp rice cereal	1 cup	250 mL
Raisins (or chopped dates)	1 cup	250 mL

(continued on the next page)

1. Grease the pan. Stir the honey and peanut butter together in the bowl. Microwave, uncovered, on high (100%) for 2 minutes until hot and bubbly. Stir in the butterscotch chips and marshmallows until melted. Microwave on medium (50%) for 30 seconds, if needed, to finish melting the marshmallows.

2. Stir in the remaining 4 ingredients. Press well in the pan. Cool. Cuts into 27 bars.

Chocolate Bar Cookies

Dotted with chocolate. Soft and chewy.

Get It Together: dry measures, medium bowl, measuring spoons, mixing spoons, thick plastic bag, rolling pin, cookie sheet, oven mitts, wire rack, waxed paper

1. Hard margarine, softened	1/2 cup	125 mL
Brown sugar, packed	1/3 cup	75 mL
Granulated sugar	1/3 cup	75 mL
2. Vanilla flavouring	1 tsp.	5 mL
Large egg, fork-beaten	1	1
3. All-purpose flour	1 1/4 cups	300 mL
Baking soda	1/2 tsp.	2 mL
Salt	1/4 tsp.	1 mL
4. Chocolate-covered buttery toffee bars (such as Skor)	2 x 1 1/2 oz.	2 x 39 g

1. Place the oven rack in the centre position. Turn the oven on to 375°F (190°C). Cream the margarine and both sugars together in the bowl until smooth.

2. Stir in the vanilla flavouring and egg.

3. Add the flour, baking soda and salt. Mix well, scraping down the sides of the bowl.

4. Place the chocolate bars in the plastic bag. Break the bars into chunky pieces by hitting them with the rolling pin. Stir the chunks into the dough. Drop by teaspoonfuls, about 2 inches (5 cm) apart, onto the ungreased cookie sheet. Bake in the oven for 10 minutes until the edges are browned. Centres will stay soft. Use the oven mitts to remove the cookie sheet to the wire rack. Let stand for 1 minute. Remove the cookies to the waxed paper to cool completely. Makes 28 cookies.

Banana Raisin Bars

Soft and chewy. These will remind you of banana bread.

Get It Together: 9 x 13 inch (23 x 33 cm) oblong baking pan, dry measures, large bowl, measuring spoons, small bowl, electric mixer, mixing spoon, oven mitts, wire rack

1.			
Quick-cooking rolled oats (not instant)	3 cups	750 mL
Long thread coconut	1 cup	250 mL
Raisins	1 cup	250 mL
Sunflower seeds	1/2 cup	125 mL
Peanuts, chopped	1/2 cup	125 mL
2. Tub margarine	1/2 cup	125 mL
Corn syrup	3 tbsp.	45 mL
Liquid honey	3 tbsp.	45 mL
Large egg	1	1
Vanilla flavouring	1 tsp.	5 mL
Mashed banana	1/3 cup	75 mL

1. Place the oven rack in the centre position. Turn the oven on to 325°F (160°C). Grease the baking pan. Combine the first 5 ingredients in the large bowl.

2. Beat the next 6 ingredients together with the electric mixer on high speed in the small bowl until light and fluffy. Stir into the rolled oat mixture and combine well. Spread in the baking pan and press down well. Bake in the oven for 50 minutes until firm and golden. Use the oven mitts to remove the baking pan to the wire rack. Cool. Cuts into 20 bars.

Pictured on page 35.

Variation: Substitute 1/2 cup (125 mL) of applesauce for the banana and add 1/8 tsp. (0.5 mL) of ground cinnamon.

Applesauce Jellied Dessert

You may want to put this dessert into four small plastic containers with lids. Then you can take it to school in your lunch bag; it will remain solid for several hours at room temperature after chilling.

Get It Together: liquid measures, medium bowl, dry measures, mixing spoon, 4 small dessert bowls

1. Package strawberry, cherry   3 oz.   85 g
   or lime-flavoured gelatin
   (jelly powder)
   Boiling water   3/4 cup   175 mL
   Applesauce, page 22, (or   1 2/3 cups   400 mL
   1 can, 14 oz., 398 mL)

1. Dissolve the gelatin in the boiling water in the bowl. Stir in the applesauce. Divide the mixture among the bowls. Chill in the refrigerator for about 3 hours. Serves 4.

Easy Raisin Cookies

This is a very easy cookie to make using a cake mix.

Get It Together: cookie sheet, liquid measures, measuring spoons, dry measures, large bowl, mixing spoon, oven mitts, wire rack, pancake lifter, waxed paper

1. Yellow cake mix, 2 layer size   1   1
   Large eggs, fork-beaten   2   2
   Cooking oil   1/3 cup   75 mL
   Water   2 tbsp.   30 mL
   Raisins   1 cup   250 mL

1. Place the oven rack in the centre position. Turn the oven on to 350°F (175°C). Grease the cookie sheet. Combine all 5 ingredients in the bowl. Stir until the cake mix is moistened and smooth. (Small lumps are fine.) Drop by tablespoonfuls onto the cookie sheet. Bake in the oven for 18 minutes until golden. Use the oven mitts to remove the cookie sheet to the wire rack. Let stand for 2 minutes. Use the pancake lifter to remove the cookies to the waxed paper on the counter. Cool completely. Makes 33 cookies.

Pictured on page 17.

Chocolate Chip Granola Bars

Chewy with chocolate and coconut. Holds together well.

Get It Together: 9 × 13 inch (23 × 33 cm) oblong baking pan, dry measures, medium bowl, mixing spoon, oven mitts, wire rack

1. | | | |
   |---|---|---|
   | Graham cracker crumbs | 1 cup | 250 mL |
   | Flaked coconut | 1 cup | 250 mL |
   | Granola | 1 1/2 cups | 375 mL |
   | Semi-sweet chocolate chips | 1 cup | 250 mL |
   | Chopped pecans (or other nuts), optional | 1/4 cup | 60 mL |

2. | | | |
   |---|---|---|
   | Sweetened condensed milk | 11 oz. | 300 mL |
   | Hard margarine, melted | 1/3 cup | 75 mL |

1. Place the oven rack in the centre position. Turn the oven on to 325°F (160°C). Grease the baking pan. Combine the first 5 ingredients in the bowl. Stir.

2. Drizzle the condensed milk and margarine over the mixture. Mix well. Press well in the baking pan. Bake in the oven for 30 minutes until lightly golden. Use the oven mitts to remove the baking pan to the wire rack. Cool. Cuts into 20 bars.

Pictured on the front cover.

Apricot Logs

Pure and natural. All fruit and coconut.

Get It Together: dry measures, measuring spoons, medium microwave-safe casserole dish, microwave oven, blender, mixing spoon, medium bowl, waxed paper, plastic wrap, sharp knife

1. | | | |
   |---|---|---|
   | Dried apricots (about 40) | 1 1/2 cups | 375 mL |
   | Water | 1 tbsp. | 15 mL |
   | Juice of 1 orange | | |

2. | | | |
   |---|---|---|
   | Grated peel of 1 orange | | |
   | Flaked coconut | 1/2 cup | 125 mL |

3. | | | |
   |---|---|---|
   | Flaked coconut | 2/3 cup | 150 mL |

(continued on the next page)

1. Put the apricots and water into the casserole dish. Cover. Microwave on high (100%) for 2 minutes until moist and plump. Put the apricot mixture and orange juice into the blender. Process, stopping the blender and stirring every few seconds, until the apricots are very finely chopped. Put the mixture into the bowl.

2. Mix in the orange peel and the first amount of coconut. Divide the mixture in half. Roll into two 6 inch (15 cm) logs.

3. Place the second amount of coconut on the waxed paper. Roll the logs in the coconut until well coated. Cover each log with plastic wrap. Place in the refrigerator to chill. Cut into 1 inch (2.5 cm) pieces. Makes 2 logs.

Pictured on page 36.

Variation: Roll the mixture into small balls rather than into logs, then roll in the coconut and chill. Makes about 18 one inch (2.5 cm) balls.

S'Mores Squares

Wow! A whole pan of s'mores! Be sure to use a hot, wet knife for cutting. These seem hard but are really just chewy.

Get It Together: 9 x 9 inch (23 x 23 cm) square baking pan, plastic bag, rolling pin, measuring spoons, dry measures, large microwave-safe bowl, waxed paper, microwave oven, mixing spoon, sharp knife

1. Whole graham crackers	48	48
2. Tub margarine	2 tbsp.	30 mL
Corn syrup	1/2 cup	125 mL
Milk (or semi-sweet) chocolate chips	1 1/2 cups	375 mL
3. Miniature marshmallows	2 cups	500 mL

1. Grease the baking pan. Put the graham crackers into the plastic bag. Coarsely crush the graham crackers with the rolling pin.

2. Place the margarine, corn syrup and chocolate chips in the bowl. Cover with waxed paper. Microwave on high (100%) for 2 minutes. Stir well. Microwave on high (100%) for 1 minute until the mixture is boiling.

3. Mix in the crushed graham crackers. Stir in the marshmallows. Press in the baking pan. Let stand at room temperature. Mixture will become quite hard and chewy. Carefully cut with the knife, dipping it in hot water after each cut. Cuts into 36 squares.

Gingerbran Cream Muffins

Cream cheese filling is the perfect touch.

Get It Together: 12 large muffin papers, muffin pan (for 12 muffins),
measuring spoons, small bowl, mixing spoon,
liquid measures, dry measures, medium bowl,
large bowl, wooden toothpick, oven mitts, wire rack

1.			
Cream cheese, softened	4 oz.	125 g
Granulated sugar	2 tbsp.	30 mL
Finely grated orange peel	1 tsp.	5 mL

2.			
Large eggs, fork-beaten	2	2
Cooking oil	1/4 cup	60 mL
Buttermilk (or reconstituted from powder)	1/2 cup	125 mL
Molasses (not blackstrap)	1/3 cup	75 mL
Natural wheat bran	1/2 cup	125 mL

3.			
All-purpose flour	1 3/4 cups	425 mL
Brown sugar, packed	1/2 cup	125 mL
Baking soda	1 tsp.	5 mL
Baking powder	1/2 tsp.	2 mL
Ground ginger	2 tsp.	10 mL
Ground allspice	1/2 tsp.	2 mL

1. Place the oven rack in the centre position. Turn the oven on to 350°F (175°C). Place the muffin papers in the pan. Combine the cream cheese, sugar and orange peel in the small bowl. Mix until smooth. Set aside.

2. Combine the next 5 ingredients in the medium bowl. Stir. Let stand for 5 minutes.

3. Combine the next 6 ingredients in the large bowl. Mix well. Make a well in the centre. Pour the milk mixture into the well. Stir just to moisten. Do not stir too much. Divide the batter among the 12 muffin cups. Gently spoon a rounded teaspoon of the cream cheese mixture into the centre of each muffin. Bake in the oven for 25 minutes until golden. The toothpick inserted in the centre of 2 or 3 muffins should come out clean. Use the oven mitts to remove the muffin pan to the wire rack. Let stand for 10 minutes. Remove the muffins from the pan to the rack to cool. Makes 12 muffins.

Pictured on page 108.

Snap Gingers

Round and flat with a chewy texture. Ginger flavour through and through.

Get It Together: dry measures, small bowl, liquid measures, mixing spoon, rubber spatula, measuring spoons, cookie sheet, drinking glass, oven mitts, wire rack, waxed paper

1. Hard margarine, softened	1/2 cup	125 mL
Granulated sugar	2/3 cup	150 mL
2. Molasses (not blackstrap)	1/4 cup	60 mL
Large egg, fork-beaten	1	1
3. All-purpose flour	1 1/2 cups	375 mL
Baking soda	1 1/2 tsp.	7 mL
Ground ginger	1 1/2 tsp.	7 mL
Salt	1/4 tsp.	1 mL
4. Granulated sugar, for coating		

1. Place the oven rack in the centre position. Turn the oven on to 375°F (190°C). Cream the margarine and first amount of sugar together well in the bowl.

2. Stir in the molasses and egg until well mixed, occasionally scraping down the sides of the bowl with the rubber spatula.

3. Stir in the next 4 ingredients until well blended.

4. Make 1 inch (2.5 cm) balls with the dough. Roll each ball in the second amount of sugar to coat. Place on the ungreased cookie sheet, 2 inches (5 cm) apart. Flatten each ball with the bottom of the glass. Bake in the oven for 7 minutes. Use the oven mitts to remove the cookie sheet to the wire rack. Let stand for 1 minute. Remove the cookies to the waxed paper to cool completely. Makes 26 cookies.

Pictured on page 107.

Did you know?

When baking muffins (or other food) in a muffin pan, if you don't use all the cups, fill the empty muffin cups halfway with water. This will prevent the muffin pan from burning.

Apple-Crisp Cookies

A nice drop cookie that keeps its shape when it bakes. Moist, with a crunch.

Get It Together: cookie sheet, dry measures, medium bowl, electric mixer, measuring spoons, mixing spoon, small bowl, oven mitts, wire rack, pancake lifter, waxed paper

1. | | | |
|---|---|---|
| Tub margarine | 2/3 cup | 150 mL |
| Brown sugar, packed | 1 cup | 250 mL |
| Large eggs, fork-beaten | 2 | 2 |
| Vanilla flavouring | 1 tsp. | 5 mL |
| Quick-cooking rolled oats (not instant) | 1 1/2 cups | 375 mL |

2. | | | |
|---|---|---|
| All-purpose flour | 1 1/2 cups | 375 mL |
| Baking powder | 1 tsp. | 5 mL |
| Ground cinnamon | 1/2 tsp. | 2 mL |
| Salt | 1/2 tsp. | 2 mL |
| Medium apples, peeled, cored and finely chopped | 2 | 2 |
| Chopped pecans (or walnuts), optional | 1/2 cup | 125 mL |

1. Place the oven rack in the centre position. Turn the oven on to 350°F (175°C). Grease the cookie sheet. Beat the margarine and sugar together on low speed in the medium bowl. Add the eggs and vanilla. Beat together well on high speed. Add the rolled oats. Stir.

2. Combine the flour, baking powder, cinnamon and salt in the small bowl. Add to the margarine mixture. Stir. Add the apple and pecans and mix well. Drop by level tablespoonfuls onto the cookie sheet. Bake in the oven for 15 minutes. Use the oven mitts to remove the cookie sheet to the wire rack. Let stand for 2 minutes. Use the pancake lifter to remove the cookies to the waxed paper on the counter. Cool completely. Makes 24 cookies.

Hot Tortilla Dip

Make this ahead and keep refrigerated. Reheat for lunch!

Get It Together: dry measures, small microwave-safe bowl, sharp knife, cutting board, paper towel, mixing spoon, measuring spoons, plastic wrap, microwave oven, oven mitts, hot pad

1. Chunky salsa   1/2 cup   125 mL
   Small tomato   1   1

2. Green onion, thinly sliced   1   1
   Dried crushed chilies   1/8 tsp.   0.5 mL

3. Process cheese loaf (such as   4 oz.   125 g
   Velveeta), cut into small cubes

4. Tortilla chips, for dipping
   Celery ribs, for dipping

1. Place the salsa in the bowl. Cut the tomato in half on the cutting board. Gently squeeze over the paper towel to remove the seeds. Discard the seeds and juice. Dice the tomato into small pieces. Stir into the salsa.

2. Add the green onion and chilies. Cover with plastic wrap. Microwave on high (100%) for 1 minute.

3. Stir cheese into the warm salsa mixture. Microwave, uncovered, on high (100%) for 30 seconds. Stir well. Repeat until the cheese is all melted. Use the oven mitts to remove the bowl to the hot pad.

4. Serve with tortilla chips and celery ribs. Makes 1 1/4 cups (300 mL).

Pictured on page 17.

Did you know?

You should never use metal pots or pans, tin foil, twist ties, lead crystal or melamine dishes or metal utensils in the microwave oven. All these products contain metal that will deflect the microwaves away from the food and could damage the microwave oven.

Honey Mustard Dunk

Great served with ham, sausages or veggies.

Get It Together: dry measures, measuring spoons, small bowl, mixing spoon

1.
Mayonnaise (or salad dressing)	**1/2 cup**	**125 mL**
Liquid honey	**2 tbsp.**	**30 mL**
Prepared mustard	**2 tsp.**	**10 mL**

1. Put all 3 ingredients into the bowl. Mix until smooth. Makes 2/3 cup (150 mL).

Pictured on the front cover.

Dilly Pickle Dip

A great dip for vegetables or Chicken Thumbs, page 42, or Spicy Chicken Fingers, page 45.

Get It Together: dry measures, small bowl, mixing spoon, measuring spoons, plastic wrap

1.
Sour cream	**1/2 cup**	**125 mL**
Plain yogurt	**1/2 cup**	**125 mL**
Finely chopped dill pickles,	**1/3 cup**	**75 mL**
blotted dry with paper towel		
Dried dillweed	**1 tsp.**	**5 mL**
Salt	**1/4 tsp.**	**1 mL**
Pepper, sprinkle		

1. Combine the sour cream and yogurt in the bowl. Stir together well. Add the remaining 4 ingredients. Stir. Cover with plastic wrap. Chill in the refrigerator for 1 hour to blend the flavours. Makes 1 1/4 cups (300 mL).

Garlic Cheese Dip

Take to school to dip fresh veggies in.

Get It Together: dry measures, measuring spoons, small bowl, mixing spoon

1. Mayonnaise (or salad dressing) — 1/2 cup — 125 mL
   Lemon juice — 1 tbsp. — 15 mL
   Garlic powder — 1/4 tsp. — 1 mL
   Onion powder — 1/8 tsp. — 0.5 mL
   Water — 1 tbsp. — 15 mL
   Grated mozzarella cheese — 1/4 cup — 60 mL
   Simulated bacon bits (or 1 bacon — 1 tbsp. — 15 mL
      slice, cooked and crumbled)

1. Combine all 7 ingredients in the bowl. Mix well. Chill in the refrigerator for 15 minutes to blend the flavours. Makes 3/4 cup (175 mL).

Garlic Mustard Dip

Put in a small container to take for lunch. Great for veggies.

Get It Together: dry measures, measuring spoons, small bowl, mixing spoon, plastic wrap

1. Mayonnaise (or salad dressing) — 1/3 cup — 75 mL
   Sour cream — 2/3 cup — 150 mL
   Prepared mustard — 1 tbsp. — 15 mL
   Garlic powder — 1/8 tsp. — 0.5 mL
   Salt, sprinkle
   Pepper, sprinkle

1. Combine all 6 ingredients in the bowl. Mix well. Cover with plastic wrap. Chill in the refrigerator for 30 minutes to blend the flavours. Store any remaining dip in the refrigerator for up to 3 days. Makes 1 1/4 cups (300 mL).

Pictured on page 35.

Choc-O-Nut Spread

Spread on graham crackers, digestive biscuits or any other whole wheat or whole grain cracker.

Get It Together: dry measures, liquid measures, measuring spoons, small bowl, mixing spoon

1. Smooth peanut butter   1/2 cup   125 mL
    Chocolate syrup   1/3 cup   75 mL
    Vanilla flavouring   1 tsp.   5 mL

1. Combine all 3 ingredients in the bowl. Mix until smooth. Makes 3/4 cup (175 mL).

Pictured on page 54.

Jam & Cheese Spread

Try spreading on bagels, or roll up in flour tortillas.

Get It Together: dry measures, small bowl, table spoon

1. Plain spreadable cream cheese   1/2 x 8 oz.   1/2 x 227 g
    (1/2 cup, 125 mL)
    Thick jam (your favourite flavour)   1/4 cup   60 mL

1. Combine the cream cheese and jam in the bowl. Mix well. Makes 3/4 cup (175 mL).

Pictured on page 143.

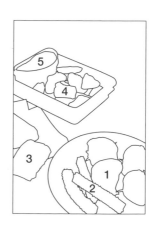

1. Vegetable Roll, page 140
2. Seeded Cheese, page 44
3. Banana Raisin Bars, page 24
4. Crispy Chicken Cracky, page 47
5. Garlic Mustard Dip, page 33

Seedy Bread Spread

Use as a spread for bagels or any other kind of bread, or as a sandwich spread instead of mayonnaise.

Get It Together: measuring spoons, medium bowl, mixing spoon

1.
Cream cheese, softened	4 oz.	125 g
Ranch (or your favourite creamy) dressing	2 tbsp.	30 mL
Finely chopped green, red or yellow pepper	2 tbsp.	30 mL
Finely grated carrot	1 tbsp.	15 mL
Finely chopped green onion	2 tbsp.	30 mL
Toasted sunflower seeds	1 tbsp.	15 mL
Cayenne pepper, sprinkle (optional)		
Salt	1/8 tsp.	0.5 mL
Pepper, sprinkle		

1. Combine all 9 ingredients in the bowl. Mix well. Makes 3/4 cup (175 mL).

1. Easy Macaroni Soup, page 136
2. Apricot Logs, page 26
3. Egg Roll Buns, page 110
4. Pepper Cheese Roll, page 106
5. Cottage Cheese Salad, page 101

Peanut Butter Pudding Dip

A great dipper for fruit, or chocolate or vanilla cookies.

Get It Together: dry measures, medium bowl, mixing spoon, liquid measures, covered container

1.	**Peanut butter**	**1/3 cup**	**75 mL**
	Milk	**2 cups**	**500 mL**
2.	**Instant vanilla pudding powder, 4 serving size**	**1**	**1**

1. Cream the peanut butter in the bowl with the spoon. Add the milk, a bit at a time, stirring together until well mixed.

2. Add the pudding powder to the peanut butter mixture. Mix for 2 minutes. Chill in the refrigerator for about 5 minutes until slightly thickened. Store any remaining dip in the covered container for up to 4 days. Makes 2 3/4 cups (675 mL).

Pictured on page 126.

PEANUT BUTTER CHOCOLATE DIP: Use instant chocolate pudding powder instead of the instant vanilla pudding powder.

PEANUT BUTTER BUTTERSCOTCH DIP: Use instant butterscotch or caramel pudding powder instead of the instant vanilla pudding powder.

PEANUT BUTTER BANANA DIP: Use instant banana pudding powder instead of the instant vanilla pudding powder.

Creamy Garlic Dip

If you like Caesar salad, you will love this dip! Great for chicken or vegetables.

Get It Together: dry measures, measuring spoons, small bowl, mixing spoon

1.

Mayonnaise (or salad dressing)	1/3 cup	75 mL
Sour cream	1/3 cup	75 mL
Garlic powder	1 tsp.	5 mL
Lemon juice	1 tbsp.	15 mL

1. Combine the mayonnaise, sour cream, garlic powder and lemon juice in the bowl. Mix well. Chill in the refrigerator for 15 minutes to blend the flavours. Makes 2/3 cup (150 mL).

Sour Cream & Onion Dip

This is a tasty dip that complements chicken or vegetables.

Get It Together: dry measures, measuring spoons, small bowl, mixing spoon, plastic wrap

1.

Sour cream	1 cup	250 mL
Plain yogurt	1/2 cup	125 mL
Minced onion flakes, crushed	2 tbsp.	30 mL
Beef bouillon powder	2 1/2 tsp.	12 mL
Worcestershire sauce	1/4 tsp.	1 mL

1. Combine all 5 ingredients in the bowl. Mix well. Cover with plastic wrap. Chill in the refrigerator for 1 hour to blend the flavours. Store any remaining dip in the refrigerator for up to 3 days. Makes 1 1/2 cups (375 mL).

Did you know?

To keep fresh vegetables cold and crisp in your lunch, place ice cubes in a plastic sandwich bag with the vegetables. Close tightly with a twist tie. Wrap in another plastic sandwich bag and fasten again with another twist tie to prevent leakage.

Smoked Salmon Spread

Spread on bread, bagels or crackers.

Get It Together: small bowl, table fork, dry measures, measuring spoons, mixing spoon, covered container

1.
Canned salmon, well drained	7 1/2 oz.	213 g
Plain spreadable cream cheese	1/3 cup	75 mL
Finely chopped celery	1 tbsp.	15 mL
Prepared horseradish	1/2 tsp.	2 mL
Liquid smoke	1/8 tsp.	0.5 mL
Onion powder	1/8 tsp.	0.5 mL

1. Mash the salmon in the bowl with the fork. Add the remaining 5 ingredients. Mix well. Ready to use. Store any remaining spread in the container in the refrigerator for up to 3 days. Makes 1 cup (250 mL).

Pictured on page 143.

Pickly Tuna Spread

Spread on bread, bagels or crackers.

Get It Together: dry measures, measuring spoons, small bowl, mixing spoon, covered container

1.
Canned tuna, drained and flaked	4 3/4 oz.	133 g
Chopped dill pickle	1/2 cup	125 mL
Chopped celery	1/2 cup	125 mL
Mayonnaise (or salad dressing)	1/3 cup	75 mL
Salt	1/8 tsp.	0.5 mL
Pepper	1/8 tsp.	0.5 mL

1. Combine all 6 ingredients in the bowl. Mix well. Ready to use. Store any remaining spread in the container in the refrigerator for up to 3 days. Makes 2 cups (500 mL).

Easy Cheese Cups

Good warm or cold. These freeze well.

Get It Together: muffin pan (for 8 muffins), dry measures, small bowl, table fork, measuring spoons, electric mixer, oven mitts, wire rack

1. Feta cheese, crumbled — 1/2 cup — 125 mL
Cottage cheese — 1/2 cup — 125 mL

2. Plain (or herbed) spreadable cream cheese — 3 tbsp. — 45 mL
Grated Parmesan (or Romano) cheese — 1 tbsp. — 15 mL
Large egg, fork-beaten — 1 — 1
Dried oregano — 1/8 tsp. — 0.5 mL
Dried basil — 1/8 tsp. — 0.5 mL
Parsley flakes — 1/4 tsp. — 1 mL
Garlic powder, sprinkle
Lemon juice — 1/2 tsp. — 2 mL

3. Tube of refrigerator crescent rolls (8 rolls per tube) — 8 1/2 oz. — 235 g

1. Place the oven rack in the centre position. Turn the oven on to 350°F (175°C). Grease 8 muffin cups. Mash the feta cheese and cottage cheese together with the fork in the bowl.

2. Add the next 8 ingredients. Beat on medium speed until smooth. Makes 1 cup (250 mL).

3. Open the crescent rolls and separate into 8 triangles. Line the muffin cups with each triangle by placing the longest side of the triangle around the top edge of the muffin cup. Press all the edges together, forming the shape of the muffin cup. Divide the creamed filling evenly among the 8 dough-lined cups. Bake in the oven for 20 to 25 minutes. Use the oven mitts to remove the muffin pan to the wire rack. Makes 8 cheese cups.

Chicken Thumbs

Good hot or cold. Great served with Dilly Pickle Dip, page 32, or Garlic Mustard Dip, page 33.

Get It Together: baking sheet, sharp knife, cutting board, measuring spoons, medium bowl, table fork, mixing spoon, dry measures, plastic freezer bag, oven mitts, wire rack

1. Boneless, skinless chicken breast halves (about 1 lb., 454 g)	4	4
2. Large egg	1	1
Milk	2 tbsp.	30 mL
Seasoning salt	1/2 tsp.	2 mL
Pepper, sprinkle		
3. Fine dry bread crumbs	3/4 cup	175 mL

1. Place the oven rack in the centre position. Turn the oven on to 400°F (200°C). Grease the baking sheet. Cut the chicken crosswise, into 1 inch (2.5 cm) pieces, on the cutting board.

2. Combine the egg and milk in the bowl. Beat with the fork until frothy. Beat in the salt and pepper. Add the chicken. Stir to coat.

3. Put the bread crumbs into the bag. Remove 6 to 7 pieces of chicken from the egg mixture with the fork, and place into the bag of crumbs. Shake until coated. Place coated chicken on the baking sheet. Repeat for all the chicken pieces. Bake in the oven for 15 to 20 minutes. Use the oven mitts to remove the baking sheet to the wire rack. Makes about 30 pieces.

Did you know?

It is important to clean the cutting board and any utensils used to cut raw chicken, fish or beef very well in hot soapy water. This will eliminate any bacteria from spreading to other food.

Nacho Skins

Zippy! Moist and very delicious. Save the scooped-out potato to fry tomorrow morning for breakfast.

Get It Together: table fork, oven mitts, wire rack, sharp knife, cutting board, table spoon, 9 x 9 inch (23 x 23 cm) square baking pan, measuring spoons, custard cup, microwave oven, pastry brush, dry measures, small bowl

1. Medium baking potatoes, with peel | 3 | 3

2. Tub margarine | 2 tbsp. | 30 mL
   Salt | 1/8 tsp. | 0.5 mL
   Cayenne pepper, sprinkle

3. Canned green chilies, drained and blotted dry with paper towel | 4 oz. | 114 mL
   Grated Cheddar cheese | 1 cup | 250 mL
   Salsa | 1/3 cup | 75 mL

4. Salsa, for dipping (optional)
   Sour cream, for dipping (optional)

1. Place the oven rack in the centre position. Turn the oven on to 425°F (220°C). Pierce the skin of each potato with the fork. Bake in the oven for 45 minutes. Use the oven mitts to remove the potatoes to the wire rack to cool. Cut each potato in half lengthwise on the cutting board. Cut each in half lengthwise again to make 4 wedges for each potato. Let cool enough to handle. Scoop out the potato from each wedge, leaving about 1/4 inch (6 mm) of potato on the skin. Place the wedges in the ungreased baking pan. Reduce the oven temperature to 350°F (175°C).

2. Place the margarine in the custard cup. Microwave on high (100%) for about 30 seconds. Stir in the salt and cayenne pepper. Brush the inside part of the potato skins with the margarine mixture.

3. Mix the green chilies with the cheese and salsa in the bowl. Spoon about 1 1/2 tbsp. (25 mL) of the mixture onto each potato skin wedge. Bake in the oven for 10 minutes until bubbling. Use the oven mitts to remove the pan to the wire rack.

4. Serve with salsa and sour cream. Makes 12 potato wedges.

Pictured on page 53 and on back cover.

Seeded Cheese

Cheese lovers will love these!

Get It Together: measuring spoons, 9 x 9 inch (23 x 23 cm) square baking pan, oven mitts, wire rack, plate, microwave-safe plate, microwave oven

1. **Sesame seeds**	2 tbsp.	30 mL
2. **Cheese (your favourite), cut into 10 sticks, 1/2 inch (12 mm) thick, 1/2 inch (12 mm) wide and about 3 inches (7.5 cm) long**	6 oz.	170 g

1. Place the oven rack in the upper position (second from the top). Turn the oven on to broil. Place the sesame seeds in the ungreased baking pan. Broil the seeds in the oven for about 3 minutes, shaking the pan occasionally using the oven mitts, until golden brown. Use the oven mitts to remove the pan to the wire rack. Put the warm seeds onto the plate.

2. Place the cheese on the microwave-safe plate. Microwave, uncovered, on high (100%) for 6 seconds until warm. Lightly press and roll the warmed cheese sticks in the seeds. Chill for 30 minutes. Makes about 10 cheese sticks.

Pictured on page 35.

Ham & Melon Kabobs

Pack in a covered container to take to school.

Get It Together: 6 wooden toothpicks

1. **Thick ham slice (about 2 oz., 57 g), cut into six 3/4 inch (2 cm) cubes**	1	1
Small cantaloupe, cut into twelve 3/4 inch (2 cm) cubes	1	1

1. Arrange 2 cubes of cantaloupe with 1 cube of ham in between on each toothpick. Makes 6 kabobs.

(continued on the next page)

Pictured on page 18.

Variation: 6 pieces of shaved ham, rolled or folded into 1 inch (2.5 cm) pieces, may be substituted for the ham cubes. The toothpick will hold the shaved ham in place.

Spicy Chicken Fingers

Great warm or cold. Serve your favourite salsa with these, or try Dilly Pickle Dip, page 32.

Get It Together: sharp knife, cutting board, measuring spoons, small bowl, table fork, dry measures, pie plate (or shallow dish), mixing spoon, 9 x 13 inch (23 x 33 cm) oblong baking pan, custard cup, microwave oven, oven mitts, wire rack

1.	**Boneless, skinless chicken breast halves (about 1 lb., 454 g)**	4	4
2.	**Large egg**	1	1
	Milk	2 tbsp.	30 mL
3.	**Cornmeal**	2/3 cup	150 mL
	Envelope of taco seasoning mix (measure about 2 1/2 tbsp., 37 mL)	1/2 x 1 1/4 oz.	1/2 x 35 g
4.	**Tub margarine**	3 tbsp.	45 mL

1. Place the oven rack in the centre position. Turn the oven on to 400°F (200°C). Cut each chicken breast into 4 pieces on the cutting board.

2. Beat the egg and milk together in the bowl with the fork until frothy.

3. Combine the cornmeal and taco seasoning in the pie plate. Stir. Dip each piece of chicken into the egg mixture and then roll in the cornmeal mixture until well coated. Place chicken in the ungreased baking pan.

4. Microwave the margarine in the custard cup on high (100%) for about 30 seconds until melted. Drizzle the chicken with the margarine. Bake in the oven for 15 minutes until crisp and golden. Use the oven mitts to remove the baking pan to the wire rack. Makes 16 pieces.

Salmon Cups

Makes a scrumptious lunch. Take these to school instead of the usual sandwich.

Get It Together: muffin pan (for 8 muffins), measuring spoons, small bowl, mixing spoon, oven mitts, wire rack

1.

Canned salmon, well drained and mashed	7.5 oz.	213 g
Finely chopped celery	2 tbsp.	30 mL
Finely sliced green onion (or 2 tsp., 10 mL, dried chives)	1 tbsp.	15 mL
Spreadable cream cheese	3 tbsp.	45 mL
Large egg, fork-beaten	1	1
Salt, sprinkle		
Pepper, sprinkle		
Dried dillweed (optional)	1/4 tsp.	1 mL

2.

Tube of refrigerator crescent rolls (8 rolls per tube)	8 1/2 oz.	235 g

1. Place the oven rack in the centre position. Turn the oven on to 350°F (175°C). Grease 8 muffin cups. Combine the first 8 ingredients in the bowl. Mix well.

2. Open the crescent rolls and separate into 8 triangles. Line the muffin cups with each triangle by placing the longest side of the triangle around the top edge of the muffin cup. Press all the edges together, forming the shape of the muffin cup. Put 2 tbsp. (30 mL) of the salmon mixture into each of the dough-lined cups. Bake for about 20 minutes until golden. Use the oven mitts to remove the muffin pan to the wire rack. Makes 8 salmon cups.

Pictured on the front cover.

Crispy Chicken Cracky

Try seasoned crackers such as vegetable-flavoured or sour cream-flavoured for a tasty treat. Serve hot or cold with Creamy Garlic Dip, page 39, Sour Cream & Onion Dip, page 39, or Garlic Mustard Dip, page 33.

Get It Together: baking sheet, sharp knife, cutting board, medium bowl, dry measures, microwave-safe bowl, microwave oven, measuring spoons, mixing spoon, plastic freezer bag, oven mitts, wire rack

1.	Boneless, skinless chicken breast halves (about 1 lb., 454 g)	4	4
2.	Tub margarine	1/4 cup	60 mL
	Worcestershire sauce (optional)	1 tsp.	5 mL
	Salt	1/2 tsp.	2 mL
	Pepper	1/4 tsp.	1 mL
3.	Soda (or your favourite) cracker crumbs, see Note	2/3 cup	150 mL

1. Place the oven rack in the centre position. Turn the oven on to 400°F (200°C). Lightly grease the baking sheet. Cut each chicken breast into 6 chunks on the cutting board. Place in the medium bowl.

2. Microwave the margarine in the microwave-safe bowl on high (100%) for about 30 seconds until melted. Add the Worcestershire sauce, salt and pepper. Drizzle the margarine mixture over the chicken. Toss to coat.

3. Put the cracker crumbs into the bag. Put 3 or 4 pieces of chicken at a time in the bag of crumbs, shaking to coat well. Place the coated chicken on the baking sheet. Bake in the oven for 18 to 20 minutes until crisp and golden. Use the oven mitts to remove the baking sheet to the wire rack. Makes 24 chunks.

Note: To make crumbs, place the crackers in a plastic freezer bag and roll with a rolling pin.

Pictured on page 35.

Pepper-Corn Crackers

A soft and chewy cracker. A perfect addition to your lunch. These freeze well.

Get It Together: dry measures, measuring spoons, medium bowl, mixing spoon, pastry blender, baking sheet, table fork, oven mitts, wire rack

1.

All-purpose flour	3/4 cup	175 mL
Cornflakes cereal	3 cups	750 mL
Baking powder	1/4 tsp.	1 mL
Grated Cheddar (or Gouda or Edam or Monterey Jack) cheese	2 cups	500 mL
Hard margarine	1/2 cup	125 mL
Finely diced red pepper	1/2 cup	125 mL

2. Paprika, sprinkle

1. Turn the oven on to 350°F (175°C). Combine the flour, cereal and baking powder in the bowl. Add the cheese. Mix well. Cut in the margarine with the pastry blender until mixture looks crumbly with pieces no bigger than the size of a small pea. The mixture should almost want to stick together. Work with your hands until a stiff dough forms. Work in the red pepper.

2. Form 1 1/2 tbsp. (25 mL) of dough into balls about 1 inch (2.5 cm) in diameter. Place the balls on the ungreased baking sheet. Flatten with the fork. Sprinkle with paprika. Bake on the centre rack in the oven for 15 minutes until golden brown. Use the oven mitts to remove the baking sheet to the wire rack. Makes 40 crackers.

Pictured on page 71.

CHILI-CORN CRACKERS: Substitute a 4 oz. (113 mL) can of well-drained green chilies for the diced red pepper.

PEPPER-ONION CRACKERS: Add 2 tbsp. (30 mL) of thinly sliced green onion at the same time as you add the red pepper.

Creamed Eggs On Toast

Prepare the sauce while the eggs are boiling.

Get It Together: small saucepan, measuring spoons, medium saucepan, dry measures, whisk, liquid measures, mixing spoon, sharp knife (or egg slicer), cutting board, toaster, table knife

1.	**Large eggs**	4	4
	Cold water		
2.	**Tub margarine**	2 tbsp.	30 mL
	All-purpose flour	1/4 cup	60 mL
	Milk	2 cups	500 mL
3.	**Onion powder**	1/4 tsp.	1 mL
	Dried chives	1/2 tsp.	2 mL
	Salt	1/2 tsp.	2 mL
	Pepper, sprinkle		
	Garlic powder, sprinkle		
4.	**Whole-wheat (or white)**	4	4
	** bread slices**		
	Tub margarine (optional)		

1. Place the eggs in the small saucepan and cover with cold water to about 1 inch (2.5 cm) higher than the eggs. Bring to a boil over high heat. Reduce the heat to medium. Simmer for 10 minutes. Remove the saucepan from the heat and pour out the water from the pan. Keep covering the eggs with cold water until they are cold. Lightly crack the shells and let the eggs sit in the water while the sauce is being made.

2. Melt the margarine in the medium saucepan over medium heat. Stir in the flour. Whisk in the milk slowly so you don't get any lumps. Bring the mixture to a boil until thickened.

3. Stir in the onion powder, chives, salt, pepper and garlic powder. Peel the eggs and chop them on the cutting board or break them up using the egg slicer in both directions. Stir into the cream sauce. Makes 2 2/3 cups (650 mL).

4. Toast the bread. Spread each slice with margarine if desired. Pour about 2/3 cup (150 mL) of egg sauce over each piece of toast to serve. Serves 4.

Spicy Taco Pie

A great all-in-one meal to do on weekends. Burst of Mexican flavours with a golden brown biscuit crust.

Get It Together: 10 inch (25 cm) glass pie plate, non-stick frying pan, mixing spoon, measuring spoons, dry measures, liquid measures, medium bowl, waxed paper, rolling pin, ruler, table spoon, oven mitts, wire rack

1.	**Lean ground beef**	1 lb.	454 g
	Canned brown beans in tomato sauce	14 oz.	398 mL
	Envelope of taco seasoning mix	1 1/4 oz.	35 g
2.	**Cornmeal**	1 tbsp.	15 mL
3.	**Biscuit mix**	2 cups	500 mL
	Milk	2/3 cup	150 mL
4.	**Grated Monterey Jack cheese**	1/2 cup	125 mL
	Grated Cheddar cheese	1/2 cup	125 mL
	Crushed corn chips	1/2 cup	125 mL
	Shredded lettuce	1 cup	250 mL
	Medium tomato, chopped	1	1
	Green onion, thinly sliced (optional)	1	1
	Sour cream	1/2 cup	125 mL

1. Place the oven rack in the centre position. Turn the oven on to 400°F (200°C). Grease the pie plate. Scramble-fry the ground beef in the frying pan over medium heat until no longer pink. Stir in the beans and taco seasoning. Reduce the heat to low. Simmer, uncovered, for 5 minutes.

2. Sprinkle cornmeal in the bottom of the pie plate.

3. Combine the biscuit mix and milk in the bowl. Stir until it forms a ball. Knead dough 7 or 8 times on a lightly floured working surface. Roll out on waxed paper into a 12 inch (30 cm) circle. Turn dough over into the pie plate. Peel off the waxed paper. Press dough lightly to form a shell. Spoon the beef mixture into the shell. Bake in the oven for 12 minutes until the crust is golden. Use the oven mitts to remove the pie plate to the wire rack.

4. Sprinkle with both cheeses, corn chips, lettuce, tomato and green onion. Place dollops of sour cream on top. Cuts into 6 wedges.

Pictured on page 53 and on back cover.

Eggs In Ham Cups

Fun way to serve ham and eggs.

Get It Together: muffin pan, oven mitts, wire rack, serving plate

1.	Round deli ham (or bologna) slices	4	4
2.	Large eggs	4	4

1. Place the oven rack in the bottom position. Turn the oven on to 350°F (175°C). Grease 4 muffin cups in the muffin pan. Fit 1 ham slice into each of the 4 muffin cups to form a shell.

2. Break 1 egg into each of the ham-lined muffin cups. Bake in the oven for 12 to 15 minutes. Use the oven mitts to remove the muffin pan to the wire rack. Remove the ham cups to the plate. Makes 4 ham cups.

Easy Oven Omelet

Great with lots of cheese.

Get It Together: deep 9 inch (23 cm) pie plate (or 1 quart, 1 L, casserole . dish), measuring spoons, medium bowl, electric mixer, dry measures, table knife, oven mitts, wire rack

1.	Large eggs	6	6
	Skim evaporated milk	13 1/2 oz.	385 mL
	All-purpose flour	1 tbsp.	15 mL
	Salt	1/4 tsp.	1 mL
2.	Grated Cheddar (or Swiss) cheese	1 1/2 cups	375 mL
	Green onions, sliced	2	2
	Medium tomato, chopped	1	1

1. Place the oven rack in the centre position. Turn the oven on to 325°F (160°C). Grease the pie plate. Beat the eggs, milk, flour and salt together on medium speed in the bowl.

2. Sprinkle the remaining 3 ingredients in the bottom of the pie plate. Pour the egg mixture gently over top. Bake in the oven for 60 to 65 minutes until the knife inserted into the centre of the omelet comes out clean. Use the oven mitts to remove the pie plate to the wire rack. Serves 4 to 6.

Pictured on page 54.

Corn Cakes

Much like a corn fritter.

Get It Together: measuring spoons, medium bowl, whisk, dry measures, mixing spoon, non-stick frying pan, pancake lifter

1.	**Large eggs**	2	2
	Seasoning salt	1/2 tsp.	2 mL
2.	**All-purpose flour**	1/3 cup	75 mL
	Baking powder	1 tsp.	5 mL
3.	**Canned kernel corn, drained**	12 oz.	341 mL
	Grated Cheddar cheese	1/3 cup	75 mL
4.	**Cooking oil**	2 tbsp.	30 mL

1. Beat the eggs and seasoning salt together in the medium bowl with the whisk.

2. Add the flour and baking powder. Whisk until smooth.

3. Add the corn and cheese. Stir to mix.

4. Heat the cooking oil in the frying pan over medium heat until hot. Drop the batter by rounded tablespoonfuls into the frying pan. Cook until golden. Turn the corn cakes over with the pancake lifter to cook the other side. Cook until golden. Makes about twelve 3 inch (7.5 cm) corn cakes.

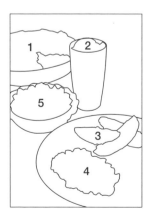

1. Spicy Taco Pie, page 50
2. Lemon Cola Float, page 20
3. Nacho Skins, page 43
4. Creamy Macaroni & Cheese, page 64
5. Bean & Tomato Salad, page 100

Quick Bread "Sandwich"

Cheese adds a nice flavour to the biscuit crust.

Get It Together: 9 inch (23 cm) pie plate, dry measures, liquid measures, measuring spoons, medium bowl, mixing spoon, table spoon, oven mitts, wire rack

1.
Biscuit mix	1 1/2 cups	375 mL
Grated sharp Cheddar cheese	1 cup	250 mL
Water	3/4 cup	175 mL
Dry mustard	1 tsp.	5 mL

2.
Shaved or chopped ham (or other deli meat)	8 oz.	225 g
Grated sharp Cheddar cheese	1 cup	250 mL
Green onions, sliced (optional)	2	2
Chopped green or red pepper	1/4 cup	60 mL

1. Place the oven rack in the centre position. Turn the oven on to 350°F (175°C). Grease the pie plate. Combine the biscuit mix, first amount of cheese, water and dry mustard in the bowl. Mix well.

2. Spread 1/2 of the batter in the pie plate. Cover with the ham, second amount of cheese, green onion and green pepper. Spread the remaining 1/2 of the batter over the top as well as you can. Bake, uncovered, in the oven for 25 to 30 minutes. Use the oven mitts to remove the pie plate to the wire rack. Serves 6 to 8.

1. Chili Fries, page 62
2. Fruity Waffles À La Mode, page 66
3. Easy Oven Omelet, page 51
4. Choco-O-Nut Spread, page 34

Kid Kwik Stir-Fry

A full meal in one bowl!

Get It Together: liquid measures, measuring spoons, mixing spoon, small cup (or bowl), non-stick frying pan with lid, dry measures, hot pad

1. | | | |
|---|---|---|
| Cold water | 1/2 cup | 125 mL |
| Cornstarch | 2 tsp. | 10 mL |
| Soy sauce | 2 tsp. | 10 mL |
| Garlic powder, sprinkle | | |

2. | | | |
|---|---|---|
| Cooking oil | 1 tsp. | 5 mL |
| Chopped fresh broccoli (or cauliflower) | 1/2 cup | 125 mL |
| Thinly sliced carrot | 1/4 cup | 60 mL |
| Medium fresh mushrooms, sliced | 2 | 2 |
| Diced cooked roast beef (or pork or chicken) | 1/2 cup | 125 mL |

3. | | | |
|---|---|---|
| Dry steam-fried noodles | 1/2 cup | 125 mL |

1. Stir the cold water, cornstarch, soy sauce and garlic powder together in the cup. Set aside.

2. Heat the cooking oil in the frying pan over medium-high heat. Stir-fry the next 4 ingredients in the hot oil for 4 to 5 minutes. Quickly stir the cornstarch mixture again and add to the vegetables in the frying pan. Cover. Cook until bubbling, thickened and clear.

3. Stir in the noodles. Cover and remove the frying pan from the heat to the hot pad. Let stand for 3 minutes. Makes 1 3/4 cups (425 mL), enough for 1 serving.

Pineapple Chicken & Rice

Sweet and sour taste, with chunky texture.

Get It Together: measuring spoons, large frying pan with lid, mixing spoon, liquid measures, dry measures, small cup

1.

Cooking oil	1 tsp.	5 mL
Lean ground chicken	1 lb.	454 g
Small onion, chopped	1	1
Large celery rib, sliced	1	1
Medium carrots, sliced	2	2
Canned pineapple chunks, with juice	14 oz.	398 mL
Hot water	2 cups	500 mL
Chicken bouillon powder	1 tbsp.	15 mL
Uncooked long-grain white rice	3/4 cup	175 mL
Chopped green or red pepper	1/2 cup	125 mL

2.

Brown sugar, packed	2 tbsp.	30 mL
White vinegar	2 tbsp.	30 mL
Ketchup	1 tbsp.	15 mL
Soy sauce	2 tsp.	10 mL

1. Heat the cooking oil in the frying pan over medium heat. Scramble-fry the ground chicken for 2 to 3 minutes. Add the onion, celery and carrot. Scramble-fry for 5 minutes until the chicken is no longer pink. Stir in the pineapple chunks with juice, hot water and bouillon powder. Bring to a boil and stir in the rice. Cover and simmer over medium-low heat for 15 minutes. Stir in the green pepper. Cover. Cook for 5 minutes until the rice is tender.

2. Combine the next 4 ingredients in the cup. Stir into the chicken rice mixture. Makes 7 cups (1.75 L).

Did you know?

If you have a microwave oven available at lunchtime, you can freeze individual servings of some finger foods or hot lunches recipes. You will be able to put these in your lunch directly from the frozen state and heat them up in the microwave oven when it's time.

Stuffed Smokie

Pack the stuffing well. Nice spicy taste.

Get It Together: sharp knife, cutting board, measuring spoons, small bowl, mixing spoon, microwave-safe plate, microwave oven

1. Smokie sausage	1	1
2. Fine dry bread crumbs	1 tbsp.	15 mL
Tub margarine, melted	1/2 tsp.	2 mL
Water	1 tsp.	5 mL
Grated Cheddar cheese	1 tbsp.	15 mL

1. Split the sausage lengthwise, part way through but not completely, on the cutting board.

2. Combine the remaining 4 ingredients in the bowl. Mix well. Pack the mixture into the split opening of the sausage and on top. Place on the plate. Microwave on high (100%) for 1 minute. Makes 1 serving.

Easy Chili

Chili is always better the next day when all the flavours have come together.

Get It Together: non-stick frying pan, mixing spoon, measuring spoons

1. Lean ground beef	1 lb.	454 g
Medium onion, chopped	1	1
Large celery rib, sliced	1	1
2. All-purpose flour	2 tbsp.	30 mL
Canned chopped stewed tomatoes, with juice	14 oz.	398 mL
Garlic powder	1/4 tsp.	1 mL
Canned kidney beans, drained	14 oz.	398 mL
Chili powder	1 tbsp.	15 mL
Granulated sugar	2 tsp.	10 mL
Paprika	1 tsp.	5 mL
Salt	1/2 tsp.	2 mL

(continued on the next page)

1. Scramble-fry the ground beef with the onion and celery in the frying pan over medium heat until the beef is no longer pink and the vegetables are tender-crisp.

2. Sprinkle the surface of the beef mixture with the flour. Stir for 1 minute. Add the remaining 7 ingredients. Bring to a boil. Cover. Simmer over low heat for 30 minutes, stirring several times. Makes 5 3/4 cups (1.45 L).

Pictured on page 71.

Spaghetti One-Dish

Nice and thick. Even the pasta is cooked in the sauce. A one-dish meal.

Get It Together: frying pan with lid, mixing spoon, measuring spoons, small bowl

1.	Lean ground beef	1/2 lb.	225 g
	Medium onion, chopped	1	1
	Medium green pepper, chopped	1/2	1/2
2.	Canned sliced mushrooms, with liquid	10 oz.	284 mL
	Canned stewed tomatoes, with juice	14 oz.	398 mL
	Can of tomato sauce	7 1/2 oz.	213 mL
	Granulated sugar	1 tsp.	5 mL
3.	Uncooked spaghetti, broken-up	4 oz.	113 g
	Grated Parmesan cheese	1 tbsp.	15 mL

1. Scramble-fry the ground beef with the onion and green pepper in the frying pan or Dutch oven over medium heat until the beef is browned and the vegetables are soft.

2. Add the mushrooms, tomatoes, tomato sauce and sugar. Cover. Bring to a boil.

3. Add the spaghetti. Stir well. Cover. Reduce the heat to medium-low. Cook for 10 minutes. Stir in the cheese just before serving. Makes 5 1/2 cups (1.4 L), enough for 2 servings.

Quick Turkey Loaf

This is perfect for sandwich meat. Slices well when cold. Freeze individual slices for your lunch.

Get It Together: 9 x 5 x 3 inch (23 x 12.5 x 7.5 cm) loaf pan, dry measures, measuring spoons, blender, large bowl, mixing spoon, oven mitts, wire rack

1.

Large egg	1	1
Ketchup	1/3 cup	75 mL
Seasoning salt	1 1/2 tsp.	7 mL
Pepper	1/8 tsp.	0.5 mL
Small onion, cut into chunks	1	1
Large carrot, peeled and cut into chunks	1	1
Large celery rib, cut into chunks	1	1

2.

Lean ground turkey (or chicken)	1 1/2 lbs.	680 g
Large flake (old-fashioned) rolled oats	2/3 cup	150 mL

1. Place the oven rack in the centre position. Turn the oven on to 350°F (175°C). Grease the loaf pan. Combine the egg, ketchup, seasoning salt and pepper in the blender. Process until smooth. While blender is processing, gradually add the onion, carrot and celery, a few at a time, through the opening in the lid. Process until almost smooth. There will be some very small chunks of vegetable remaining.

2. Put the ground turkey into the bowl. Pour the vegetable mixture over. Mix well. Stir in the rolled oats and let stand for 10 minutes. Pack into the loaf pan. Bake in the oven for 1 1/4 hours. Use the oven mitts to remove the pan to the wire rack. Let stand for 5 minutes. Cuts into 10 to 12 slices.

Pictured on page 72.

Creamy Beef 'N' Pasta

Much like stroganoff. Easy because it's made in one dish.

Get It Together: large frying pan with lid, mixing spoon, measuring spoons, liquid measures, dry measures, oven mitts, hot pad

1.	Lean ground beef	1 lb.	454 g
	Medium onion, chopped	1	1
2.	Seasoning salt	1 tsp.	5 mL
	Pepper	1/8 tsp.	0.5 mL
	Beef bouillon powder	1 tbsp.	15 mL
	Hot water	1 1/2 cups	375 mL
	Canned sliced mushrooms, with liquid	10 oz.	284 mL
	Condensed cream of mushroom soup	10 oz.	284 mL
	Uncooked elbow macaroni (or small shell pasta)	1 cup	250 mL
3.	Sour cream	1/2 cup	125 mL

1. Scramble-fry the ground beef in the frying pan over medium heat for about 3 minutes. Add the onion. Scramble-fry until the beef is browned and the onion is soft. Drain off fat.

2. Sprinkle the beef mixture with the seasoning salt, pepper and bouillon powder. Pour in the hot water, mushrooms and mushroom soup. Bring mixture to a boil. Stir in the macaroni. Cover and reduce the heat to medium-low. Cook for 15 minutes, stirring once or twice until the macaroni is tender.

3. Use the oven mitts to remove the frying pan to the hot pad. Stir in the sour cream. Makes 6 cups (1.5 L), enough for 2 servings.

Doctored Beans

A great source of protein. A delicious old-fashioned favourite.

Get It Together: dry measures, measuring spoons, 1 quart (1 L) microwave-safe dish with lid, microwave oven, mixing spoon

1.
Canned baked brown beans in molasses (or in tomato sauce)	14 oz.	398 mL
Diced cooked ham	1/2 cup	125 mL
Ketchup	1 tsp.	5 mL
Prepared mustard	1 tsp.	5 mL
Brown sugar, packed	1 tsp.	5 mL
Onion powder	1/8 tsp.	0.5 mL

1. Combine all 6 ingredients in the dish. Cover. Microwave on high (100%) for 2 minutes. Stir. Cover. Microwave for 2 minutes. Let stand for 2 minutes before serving. Makes 1 3/4 cups (425 mL).

Chili Fries

Just like the ones you would get in a fast-food restaurant—only better!

Get It Together: non-stick frying pan, mixing spoon, dry measures, measuring spoons, 9 x 13 inch (23 x 33 cm) oblong baking pan, oven mitts, wire rack

1.
Lean ground beef	1 lb.	454 g
Chopped onion	1 cup	250 mL
Finely chopped celery	2 cups	500 mL

2.
All-purpose flour	1 tbsp.	15 mL
Canned kidney beans, drained	14 oz.	398 mL
Seasoning salt	1 tsp.	5 mL
Pepper	1/8 tsp.	0.5 mL
Chili powder	1 1/2 tsp.	7 mL
Can of tomato sauce	7 1/2 oz.	213 mL
Ketchup	1/4 cup	60 mL

3.
Frozen french fries (1/2 x 2.2 lbs., 1/2 x 1 kg., package)	4 cups	1 L

(continued on the next page)

1. Place the oven rack in the centre position. Turn the oven on to 425°F (220°C). Scramble-fry the ground beef in the frying pan over medium heat for 3 minutes. Add the onion and celery. Scramble-fry until the beef is no longer pink and the onion is soft.

2. Sprinkle with the flour. Stir well. Add the next 6 ingredients. Mix well. Bring to a boil. Pour into the ungreased pan.

3. Top with the french fries. Bake in the oven for 25 to 30 minutes. Use the oven mitts to remove the pan to the wire rack. Serves 6.

Pictured on page 54.

Macaroni & Cottage Cheese

A new twist to an old favourite.

Get It Together: liquid measures, measuring spoons, medium saucepan, dry measures, mixing spoon, colander, frying pan

1.			
Water		4 cups	1 L
Salt		1 tsp.	5 mL
Uncooked elbow macaroni		1 1/2 cups	375 mL
(or small shell pasta)			

2.			
Tub margarine		2 tsp.	10 mL
Finely chopped onion		1/3 cup	75 mL
Simulated bacon bits (or		1 tbsp.	15 mL
slice, cooked crisp			
and crumbled)			
Cottage cheese		1 1/4 cups	300 mL
Salt, sprinkle			
Pepper, sprinkle			

1. Bring the water and first amount of salt to a boil in the saucepan. Add the macaroni. Cook, stirring occasionally, for 7 to 9 minutes until just tender. Drain pasta in the colander. Rinse with hot water and drain again. Return the pasta to the saucepan. Cover to keep warm.

2. Melt the margarine in the frying pan. Add the onion and cook, stirring often, until soft and golden. Add the bacon bits. Pour the onion mixture over the pasta. Stir in the cottage cheese. Sprinkle with the second amount of salt and pepper. Makes 4 cups (1 L).

Pictured on page 90.

Creamy Macaroni & Cheese

Make this delicious homemade version.

Get It Together: measuring spoons, small saucepan, dry measures, 2 mixing spoons, liquid measures, large saucepan, colander

1.

Tub margarine	1 tbsp.	15 mL
Chopped onion	1/4 cup	60 mL

2.

All-purpose flour	1 1/2 tbsp.	25 mL
Skim evaporated milk	1 cup	250 mL
Grated Cheddar cheese	1/2 cup	125 mL
Process Cheddar cheese slices	2	2
Salt	1/4 tsp.	1 mL
Pepper, sprinkle		
Dry mustard (or paprika), optional	3/4 tsp.	4 mL

3.

Water	8 cups	2 L
Elbow macaroni (or small shell pasta)	1 cup	250 mL

1. Melt the margarine over medium heat in the small saucepan. Cook the onion, stirring often, until soft.

2. Stir in the flour. Gradually add the milk, stirring constantly, until boiling. Stir in the cheeses, salt, pepper and dry mustard. Stir until the cheese is melted. Remove from the heat.

3. Measure the water into the large saucepan. Bring to a boil. Stir in the macaroni. Cook for 5 to 6 minutes until the pasta is just tender. Drain in the colander. Place in the saucepan. Add the cheese sauce to the pasta. Stir well. Makes 4 cups (1 L).

Note: This can be made ahead of time and rewarmed in a 350°F (175°C) oven in a 1 quart (1 L) casserole dish for 30 to 40 minutes.

Pictured on page 53 and on back cover.

Two-Potato Pancakes

These are delicious and a nice change from the usual lunch.

Get It Together: colander, 4 paper towels, dry measures, measuring spoons, medium bowl, mixing spoon, frying pan, pancake lifter

1. | | | |
   |---|---|---|
   | **Medium baking potatoes, peeled and grated** | 2 | 2 |
   | **Chopped onion** | 1/3 cup | 75 mL |
   | **All-purpose flour** | 1 tbsp. | 15 mL |
   | **Large egg, fork-beaten** | 1 | 1 |
   | **Salt** | 1/4 tsp. | 1 mL |
   | **Pepper, sprinkle** | | |

2. | | | |
   |---|---|---|
   | **Cooking oil** | 1 1/2 tsp. | 7 mL |

3. **Applesauce (or sour cream), for garnish**

1. Rinse the grated potato with cold water in the colander. Dry between the paper towels. Combine the potato with the next 5 ingredients in the bowl. Mix well.

2. Heat the cooking oil in the frying pan over medium heat. Drop heaping 1/4 cup (60 mL) measures of potato mixture into the frying pan, forming individual potato pancakes. Cook for 5 minutes until golden brown. Turn the pancakes over with the pancake lifter to cook the other side. Cook for 5 minutes until golden brown.

3. Serve with applesauce or sour cream. Makes 10 pancakes.

Did you know?

When dry bread crumbs are needed in a recipe, use stale (or 2-day-old) white or whole-wheat bread. Using fresh bread will make the crumbs soggy. Remove the crusts from the bread. Cut or break into pieces, then blend or process until fine crumbs form. Store bread crumbs in an airtight container or in a sealable plastic bag. Bread crumbs can also be frozen.

Fruit Waffles À La Mode

As delicious as cherry pie. Use a variety of pie fillings for different tastes. Try peach or raisin. Gets top marks for presentation and eye appeal.

Get It Together: baking sheet, dry measures, table spoon, oven mitts, wire rack, pancake lifter, luncheon plates, ice-cream scoop

1. Frozen plain (or buttermilk) waffles	2	2
2. Canned cherry pie filling	1/2 cup	125 mL
3. Small scoops of vanilla ice cream	2	2

1. Place the oven rack in the centre position. Turn the oven on to 350°F (175°C). Place both waffles on the ungreased baking sheet.

2. Spoon 1/4 cup (60 mL) of pie filling onto each waffle. Bake in the oven for 20 minutes until the pie filling is hot and bubbling and the waffle is crisp. Use the oven mitts to remove the baking sheet to the wire rack. Use the pancake lifter to place the waffles on the plates.

3. Top each hot waffle with 1 scoop of ice cream. Makes 2 waffles.

Pictured on page 54.

Broccoli-Sauced Potatoes

Thick and creamy broccoli sauce in every mouthful.

Get It Together: table fork, measuring spoons, sharp knife, oven mitts, wire rack, dry measures, liquid measures, medium saucepan, colander, mixing spoon, luncheon plates

1. Medium potatoes, with peel	4	4
Cooking oil	1 tsp.	5 mL
2. Chopped broccoli, fresh or frozen	2 cups	500 mL
Water	1/2 cup	125 mL

(continued on the next page)

3.	Tub margarine	2 tbsp.	30 mL
	Chopped onion	1/4 cup	60 mL
	All-purpose flour	3 tbsp.	45 mL
	Milk	1 cup	250 mL
4.	Process Swiss cheese slices	4	4
	(or your favourite), cut into		
	small pieces		
	Ground nutmeg, sprinkle		
	Seasoning salt	1/2 tsp.	2 mL
	Pepper, sprinkle		

1. Place the oven rack in the centre position. Turn the oven on to 425°F (220°C). Wash the potatoes well. Poke 3 or 4 times with the fork. Coat your hands with the cooking oil and rub the potatoes all over. Bake in the oven for 45 to 50 minutes until tender when pierced with the knife. Use the oven mitts to remove the potatoes to the wire rack.

2. Put the broccoli into the water in the saucepan. Bring to a boil. Reduce the heat to low. Cover and simmer for 5 minutes until tender. Remove from the heat. Drain well in the colander. Set aside.

3. Melt the margarine in the same saucepan over medium heat. Cook the onion, stirring often, until soft. Sprinkle the flour over the onion. Mix well. Gradually stir in the milk, stirring continually, until the sauce is boiling and thickened.

4. Stir the cheese into the hot sauce. Add nutmeg, seasoning salt and pepper. Stir until the cheese is melted. Add the broccoli. Stir. Cut the potatoes in half and place on individual plates. Fluff up the insides with the fork. Spoon about 1/4 cup (60 mL) of broccoli sauce over each potato half. Makes 2 1/2 cups (625 mL) broccoli sauce, enough for 8 potato halves.

Pictured on page 144.

Mexican Potato Casserole

Very tasty! Make ahead and reheat when you're ready for lunch.

Get It Together: 1 1/2 quart (1.5 L) casserole dish, measuring spoons, custard cup, microwave oven, mixing spoon, sharp knife, non-stick frying pan, dry measures, table spoon, oven mitts, wire rack

1. Medium potatoes, with peel, cut into bite-size chunks — 3 — 3

2. Tub margarine — 2 tbsp. — 30 mL
   Envelope of taco seasoning mix (measure about 2 1/2 tbsp., 37 mL) — 1/2 x 1 1/4 oz. — 1/2 x 35 g

3. Lean ground beef — 1/2 lb. — 225 g
   Chopped onion — 1/4 cup — 60 mL
   Salsa — 1 cup — 250 mL
   Chopped green pepper — 1/2 cup — 125 mL

4. Grated Monterey Jack cheese — 1 cup — 250 mL

1. Place the oven rack in the centre position. Turn the oven on to 425°F (220°C). Lightly grease the casserole dish. Place the potatoes in the casserole dish.

2. Place the margarine in the custard cup. Microwave on high (100%) for 30 to 50 seconds until melted. Stir in the taco seasoning. Pour over the potatoes. Stir to coat well. Bake, uncovered, in the oven for 40 minutes. Stir. Bake for about 10 minutes until the potatoes feel soft when poked with the knife.

3. Scramble-fry the ground beef in the frying pan over medium-high heat for 3 minutes. Add the onion. Scramble-fry until the beef is no longer pink and the onion is soft. Remove from the heat. Drain off fat. Stir in the salsa and green pepper.

4. Spoon the beef mixture over the potato in the casserole dish. Top with the cheese. Bake, uncovered, in the oven for 10 minutes. Use the oven mitts to remove the casserole dish to the wire rack. Serves 4.

Simple Sloppy Joes

Serve over toast, toasted bun halves, or inside slightly hollowed-out buns.

Get It Together: non-stick frying pan, mixing spoon, colander,
measuring spoons, dry measures

1.	Lean ground beef	1 lb.	454 g
2.	Condensed tomato soup	10 oz.	284 mL
	Ketchup	2 tbsp.	30 mL
	Prepared mustard	1 tbsp.	15 mL
	Sweet pickle relish	1/4 cup	60 mL

1. Scramble-fry the ground beef in the frying pan over medium heat until browned and no longer pink. Drain off fat.

2. Stir in the next 4 ingredients. Simmer, uncovered, over low heat for 20 minutes. Makes 2 cups (500 mL).

Broccoli 'N' Rice

Get your starch, vegetable and protein all together in this dish.

Get It Together: dry measures, measuring spoons, liquid measures,
1 quart (1 L) casserole dish, microwave oven,
mixing spoon, oven mitts, hot pad

1.	Uncooked instant white rice	1/2 cup	125 mL
	Minced onion flakes	1 tbsp.	15 mL
	Water	1/2 cup	125 mL
	Chopped fresh broccoli	2 cups	500 mL
	Condensed cream of celery soup	10 oz.	284 mL
	Salt	1/2 tsp.	2 mL
	Pepper, sprinkle		
2.	Process Cheddar cheese slices, cut into small pieces	4	4

1. Layer the first 7 ingredients, in order given, in the casserole dish. Cover. Microwave on high (100%) for 5 minutes. Stir. Cover and cook for 5 minutes. Use the oven mitts to remove the casserole dish to the hot pad.

2. Stir the cheese into the rice mixture. Cover. Let stand for 2 minutes. Stir. Makes 5 cups (1.25 L).

Make-Ahead Cheese Toast

This is a great lunch for weekends. Surprise your family and make this for them. Prepare it the night before and simply pop it in the oven the next day when ready to eat.

Get It Together: 9 x 9 inch (23 x 23 cm) square baking pan, bread knife, measuring spoons, small bowl, table fork, liquid measures, plastic wrap, oven mitts, wire rack

1. White (or whole-wheat)   8   8
       bread slices, crusts removed
Cheddar cheese slices, to cover

2. Large eggs   2   2
Prepared mustard   2 tsp.   10 mL
Salt   1/4 tsp.   1 mL
Milk   1/2 cup   125 mL
Paprika, sprinkle

1. Lightly grease the baking pan. Cover the bottom of the baking pan with 4 of the bread slices, trimming to fit. Top with the cheese. Cover with the remaining 4 bread slices, trimming to fit.

2. Beat the eggs, mustard and salt together in the bowl with the fork. Add the milk. Mix well. Pour evenly over the bread, making sure all the bread is covered. Sprinkle with paprika. Cover with plastic wrap and chill in the refrigerator for 2 hours or overnight. Place the oven rack in the centre position. Turn the oven on to 350°F (175°C). Bake, uncovered, for 30 minutes. Use the oven mitts to remove the baking pan to the wire rack. Let stand for 2 or 3 minutes until set. Serves 4.

1. Easy Chili, page 58
2. Pepper-Corn Crackers, page 48
3. Fruity Banana Meatballs, page 78
4. Pizza Pinwheels, page 84

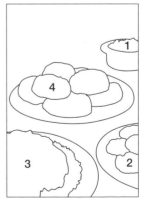

Loaded Quesadilla

Pronounced keh-sah-DEE-yah. This recipe can be increased to make as many quesadillas as you want.

Get It Together: baking sheet with sides, measuring spoons, table knife, dry measures, oven mitts, wire rack, sharp knife

1.

White (or whole-wheat) flour tortilla (10 inch, 25 cm, size)	1	1
Salsa	2 tbsp.	30 mL
Grated Cheddar (or Monterey Jack) cheese (or a mixture of both)	1/3 cup	75 mL
Bacon slice, cooked crisp and crumbled	1	1
Finely chopped fresh vegetables (such as broccoli, green peppers, green onion or jalapeño peppers)	6 tbsp.	100 mL

1. Place the oven rack in the centre position. Turn the oven on to 400°F (200°C). Lay the tortilla flat on the baking sheet. Spread the salsa over one half of the tortilla. Sprinkle the cheese, bacon and vegetables over the salsa. Fold the plain half of the tortilla over the topped side. Bake for 5 to 8 minutes until the cheese is melted and the edges are crispy. Use the oven mitts to remove the baking sheet to the wire rack. Cut into wedges to eat. Makes 1 quesadilla.

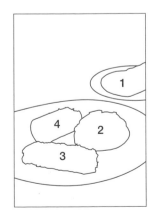

Stuffed Potato Boats

These potato boats can be wrapped and frozen. Microwave on high (100%) for one minute if the potato is thawed, or microwave, covered, on high (100%) for two and one-half to three minutes if frozen.

Get It Together: table fork, microwave oven, sharp knife, cutting board, table spoon, small bowl, measuring spoons, dry measures, microwave-safe plate

1. **Medium potato, with peel** — 1 — 1

2.
Tub margarine	2 tsp.	10 mL
Onion salt	1/4 tsp.	1 mL
Pepper, sprinkle		
Grated Parmesan cheese	1 tbsp.	15 mL
Sour cream	1/4 cup	60 mL
Grated Cheddar cheese	1/4 cup	60 mL

3. **Paprika, sprinkle**

1. Poke the potato several times with the fork. Microwave on high (100%) for 4 minutes, turning the potato over after 2 minutes. Let it stand for 2 minutes. Using the knife, cut the potato in half, lengthwise, on the cutting board. Using the spoon, scoop out the potato pulp from the centres, leaving the skins about 1/4 inch (6 mm) thick.

2. Mash the potato pulp well in the bowl with the fork. Add the margarine, onion salt, pepper, Parmesan cheese and sour cream. Stuff each potato shell with 1/2 of the mashed mixture. Place on the plate. Sprinkle with the Cheddar cheese.

3. Sprinkle each stuffed potato with paprika. Microwave on high (100%) for 2 minutes until hot and cheese is melted. Makes 2 potato boats.

Ham Stacks

Very quick and easy. The sauce is tasty with a hint of cloves.

Get It Together: paper towel, liquid measures, measuring spoons, pie plate (or shallow dish), mixing spoon, frying pan, pancake lifter, serving plate

1.

Maraschino cherries	4	4
Canned sliced pineapple rings, drained, 1/2 cup (125 mL) juice reserved	4	4

2.

Reserved pineapple juice		
Brown sugar, packed	2 tbsp.	30 mL
Ground ginger	1/4 tsp.	1 mL
Ground cloves, sprinkle		
Baked round ham slices, cut 1/4 inch (6 mm) thick (about 10 oz., 285 g)	4	4

3.

Tub margarine	1 tsp.	5 mL

4.

Cornstarch	2 tsp.	10 mL

1. Dry the cherries and pineapple slices on the paper towel.

2. Stir the pineapple juice, sugar, ginger and cloves together in the pie plate. Place the ham slices in the juice mixture, turning each slice several times to coat.

3. Melt 1/2 tsp. (2 mL) of the margarine in the frying pan over medium heat. Remove the ham from the juice mixture and place in the frying pan. Cook the ham for 5 minutes until golden. Turn the ham over with the pancake lifter to cook the other side. Cook for 5 minutes until golden. Remove the ham slices to the serving plate. Melt the remaining 1/2 tsp. (2 mL) of the margarine in the frying pan. Cook the pineapple slices for 3 minutes on each side. Place 1 pineapple slice on top of each ham slice. Place a cherry in the centre of each pineapple slice. Keep warm.

4. Stir the cornstarch into the remaining juice mixture in the pie plate. Pour into the frying pan. Stir until the sauce is bubbling and thickened. Drizzle 1 tbsp. (15 mL) of the sauce over each decorated ham slice. Serves 4.

Pictured on page 144.

Sausage & Apple Bake

Cut the sausage with a wet knife to help avoid the build-up of meat. Wash the knife off if it does.

Get It Together: frying pan, mixing spoon, dry measures, liquid measures, measuring spoons, small bowl

1. Pork (or pork and beef)
sausages, cut crosswise into
1/2 inch (12 mm) rounds

Pork (or pork and beef) sausages, cut crosswise into 1/2 inch (12 mm) rounds	1 lb.	454 g
Large apple, cored and diced	1	1
Diced onion	1/4 cup	60 mL

2.
Apple juice	2 cups	500 mL
Brown sugar, packed	1/4 cup	60 mL
Ground cinnamon	1/8 tsp.	0.5 mL
Cornstarch	2 1/2 tbsp.	37 mL

1. Scramble-fry the sausage in the frying pan over medium heat for 2 minutes. Add the apple and onion. Stir and cook until onion is soft and the mixture is starting to brown.

2. Pour in the apple juice. Combine the remaining 3 ingredients in the bowl. Stir into the apple juice mixture. Bring to a boil to thicken slightly. Makes 5 cups (1.25 L).

Variation: Omit the cinnamon and use 1/4 tsp. (1 mL) of maple flavouring.

Pineapple Cheese Waffles

A boost in flavour to ordinary frozen waffles.

Get It Together: dry measures, small bowl, table fork, measuring spoons, table knife, baking sheet, oven mitts, wire rack

1.
Cottage cheese	1/2 cup	125 mL

2.
Brown sugar, packed	2 tsp.	10 mL
Ground cinnamon	1/8 tsp.	0.5 mL
Frozen plain (or buttermilk) waffles	2	2

3.
Canned pineapple slices, drained very well on paper towel	2	2

(continued on the next page)

1. Place the oven rack in the centre position. Turn the oven on to 350°F (175°C). Put the cottage cheese into the bowl. Mash with the fork until smooth and creamy.

2. Add the sugar and cinnamon. Spread the cheese mixture over the frozen waffles. Place on the ungreased baking sheet.

3. Lay the pineapple slices over the cheese mixture. Bake in the oven for 20 minutes until the cheese is hot and the waffle is crispy. Use the oven mitts to remove the baking sheet to the wire rack. Serve immediately. Makes 2 waffles.

Peanutty Pasta Sauce

Serve over pasta or, for a change, steamed vegetables. Also makes a good dipping sauce for chicken nuggets.

Get It Together: measuring spoons, frying pan, mixing spoon, dry measures, liquid measures, whisk, small cup

1.	Cooking oil	2 tsp.	10 mL
	Small onion, chopped	1	1
	Garlic powder	1 1/4 tsp.	6 mL
2.	Peanut butter	1/2 cup	125 mL
	Apple juice	3 tbsp.	45 mL
	Soy sauce	1 1/2 tbsp.	25 mL
	Ground ginger	1 tsp.	5 mL
	Pepper	1/4 tsp.	1 mL
	Water	1 1/2 cups	375 mL
3.	Evaporated milk	1/4 cup	60 mL
	Cornstarch	2 tsp.	10 mL

1. Heat the cooking oil in the frying pan over medium heat. Cook the onion in the oil, stirring often, for 2 minutes. Sprinkle with the garlic powder. Cook for 1 minute.

2. Stir in the peanut butter and apple juice until smooth. Whisk in the soy sauce, ginger, pepper and water. Bring to a boil.

3. Combine the milk and cornstarch in the cup. Slowly stir into the boiling sauce. Cook for 2 minutes until thickened. If not using immediately, store, covered, in the refrigerator. Makes 2 2/3 cups (650 mL).

Fruity Banana Meatballs

The fruit sauce is great served over rice. This is a delicious hot lunch.

Get It Together: 2 1/2 quart (2.5 L) casserole dish, dry measures, measuring spoons, medium bowl, mixing spoon, small bowl, sharp knife, cutting board, oven mitts, wire rack, serving platter

1.			
Ground pork and beef mix (or 1/2 lb., 225 g, each of ground pork and ground beef)	1 lb.	454 g
Finely chopped onion	1/3 cup	75 mL
Seasoning salt	1/2 tsp.	2 mL
Garlic powder	1/8 tsp.	0.5 mL
Large egg, fork-beaten	1	1
Fine dry bread crumbs	1/3 cup	75 mL

2.			
Canned fruit cocktail, with juice	14 oz.	398 mL
Lemon juice	2 tbsp.	30 mL
Brown sugar, packed	3 tbsp.	45 mL
Cornstarch	1 tbsp.	15 mL
Curry powder	1/2 tsp.	2 mL
Firm medium bananas, peeled	2	2

3.			
Hot cooked rice (or couscous)	4 cups	1 L

1. Place the oven rack in the centre position. Turn the oven on to 400°F (200°C). Grease the casserole dish. Combine the first 6 ingredients in the medium bowl. Mix well. Form into 1 inch (2.5 cm) balls. Place in a single layer in the casserole dish. Bake, uncovered, in the oven for 20 minutes. Drain off fat.

2. Combine the next 5 ingredients in the small bowl. Cut the banana into 1/2 inch (12 mm) thick slices on the cutting board. Stir into the fruit cocktail mixture. Pour over the meatballs. Cover. Bake for 30 minutes until bubbling and the banana is softened, but not mushy. Use the oven mitts to remove the casserole dish to the wire rack.

3. Arrange the rice on the platter. Spoon the meatballs and sauce over the rice to serve. Makes about 24 meatballs and 2 1/3 cups (575 mL) fruit sauce.

Pictured on page 71.

Poutine

Pronounced poo-TIN. Try this delicious French-Canadian dish today!

Get It Together: 9 x 13 inch (23 x 33 cm) oblong baking pan, oven mitts, wire rack, pancake lifter, liquid measures, measuring spoons, jar with lid, small saucepan, mixing spoon, dry measures

1. Frozen french fries (1/2 x 2.2 lbs., 1/2 x 1 kg, package) — 4 cups — 1 L

2.

Water	1 cup	250 mL
All-purpose flour	2 tbsp.	30 mL
Beef bouillon powder	2 tsp.	10 mL
Onion powder	1/4 tsp.	1 mL
Seasoning salt	1/4 tsp.	1 mL
Pepper, sprinkle		
Liquid gravy browner (optional)		

3. Grated mozzarella cheese — 1 cup — 250 mL

1. Place the oven rack in the bottom position. Turn the oven on to 450°F (230°C). Place the frozen fries in the ungreased pan. Bake for 10 minutes. Use the oven mitts to remove the pan to the wire rack. Mix the fries, turning them over with the pancake lifter. Return the pan to the oven. Bake for 10 minutes. Use the oven mitts to remove the pan to the wire rack.

2. Put the water and flour into the jar. Fit the lid on tightly. Shake the jar until flour mixture appears to be smooth. Pour the mixture into the saucepan. Add the bouillon powder, onion powder, seasoning salt and pepper. Stir over medium heat until the sauce is bubbling and slightly thickened. Add the gravy browner if desired. Pour the sauce over the hot fries in the pan.

3. Top with the cheese. Bake for 2 minutes until the cheese is melted. Serves 4.

Mushroom Swiss Potato

A hearty stuffed potato that is quick to make (and nutritious).

Get It Together: table fork, paper towel, microwave oven, oven mitts, cutting board, measuring spoons, frying pan, mixing spoon, sharp knife, table spoon

1. Large potato, with peel   1   1

2. Tub margarine   2 tsp.   10 mL
   Large mushrooms, sliced   4   4

3. Garlic powder, sprinkle
   Pepper, sprinkle
   Salt, sprinkle

4. Process Swiss cheese slice,   1-2   1-2
   broken into pieces

1. Poke the potato 3 or 4 times with the fork. Wrap in the paper towel and microwave on high (100%) for 7 minutes. Use the oven mitts to remove the potato to the cutting board to finish cooking.

2. Melt the margarine in the frying pan over medium heat. Add the mushrooms. Cook for 1 minute.

3. Add the next 3 ingredients and cook, stirring often, until the mushrooms are golden.

4. Cut a large X in the top of the potato, going in about 1 inch (2.5 cm). Push the bottom sides inward to open the X slightly. Lay the pieces of cheese on the potato and spoon the mushrooms over the top. Microwave on high (100%) for 30 to 40 seconds to melt the cheese. Makes 1 large stuffed potato.

Pictured on page 72.

Did you know?

Cleaning the microwave oven is a snap. Simply put a glass of water in the microwave oven. Heat on high (100%) for 2 1/2 to 3 minutes until boiling and steaming. Use oven mitts to remove the glass of water. Wipe the walls with a damp dish cloth, then clean and shine them with a tea towel.

Pass-Da Pizza

The pasta makes the crust of the pizza. Very delicious.

Get It Together: deep-dish 12 inch (30 cm) pizza pan, liquid measures, measuring spoons, medium saucepan, mixing spoon, colander, table fork, oven mitts, wire rack

1. Water | 8 cups | 2 L
Salt | 1 tsp. | 5 mL
Cooking oil (optional) | 1 tsp. | 5 mL
Spaghettini (or vermicelli) pasta | 6 oz. | 170 g

2. Large egg | 1 | 1
Milk | 2 tbsp. | 30 mL

3. Spaghetti sauce (your | 1 1/2 cups | 375 mL
   favourite kind)
Sliced pepperoni (or other | 3/4 cup | 175 mL
   spicy) sausage
Grated mozzarella cheese | 1 1/2 cups | 375 mL
Thinly sliced green pepper
   (or onion or mushrooms),
   to cover (optional)
Grated Parmesan cheese (optional) | 1/4 cup | 60 mL

1. Place the oven rack in the centre position. Turn the oven on to 350°F (175°C). Grease the pizza pan. Combine the water, salt and cooking oil in the saucepan. Stir. Bring to a boil. Add the pasta. Boil, uncovered, for 6 to 8 minutes until just tender. Drain the pasta in the colander. Rinse with cold water. Drain.

2. In the same saucepan, beat the egg and milk together with the fork. Return the pasta to the saucepan. Mix well. Turn into the pizza pan. Spread evenly.

3. Spread the spaghetti sauce on top. Sprinkle with the pepperoni, mozzarella cheese and green pepper. Top with the Parmesan cheese. Bake in the oven for 30 minutes. Use the oven mitts to remove the pizza pan to the wire rack. Let stand for 5 minutes. Cuts into 10 wedges.

Pictured on page 144.

Garden Pitas

The colour and taste of a garden of vegetables.

Get It Together: baking sheet, measuring spoons, table knife, dry measures, oven mitts, wire rack

1.	**Mashed salsa (or pizza sauce)**	2 tbsp.	30 mL
	Pita bread (8 inch, 20 cm, size)	1	1
2.	**Grated carrot**	1 tbsp.	15 mL
	Finely chopped green or red pepper	1 tbsp.	15 mL
	Finely chopped green onion	1 tbsp.	15 mL
	Diced tomato	2 tbsp.	30 mL
	Grated mozzarella cheese	1/4 cup	60 mL

1. Place the oven rack in the upper position. Turn the oven on to broil. Lay the pita bread on the ungreased baking sheet. Spread the salsa over the pita bread.

2. Sprinkle the remaining 5 ingredients over the salsa. Broil in the oven until the cheese is melted and the edges are crisp and browned. Use the oven mitts to remove the baking sheet to the wire rack. Cuts into 6 wedges.

Did you know?

When broiling, take extra care and caution when it comes to the cooking time stated in the recipe. Watch carefully because food cooks very fast when close to the heating element in the oven.

Pizza Thingies

These individual pizzas may be wrapped well and frozen then thawed before baking. Wonderfully convenient for a hot lunch at home or bake and freeze for your lunch bag. They will be defrosted by lunch, then just heat in microwave oven for 30 to 60 seconds.

Get It Together: frying pan, stirring spoon, dry measures, hot pad, measuring spoons, table knife, baking sheet, oven mitts, wire rack

1.			
Bacon, diced	1 lb.	454 g
Sliced fresh mushrooms	2 cups	500 mL

2.			
Ketchup	1 cup	250 mL
Green onions, sliced	2	2
Worcestershire sauce	2 tsp.	10 mL
Dried oregano	1/2 tsp.	2 mL
Dry mustard	1/2 tsp.	2 mL

3.			
Process cheese spread	1/3 cup	75 mL
Hamburger buns (or any other type), split in half	6	6
Grated mozzarella cheese	2/3 cup	150 mL

1. Place the oven rack in the bottom position. Turn the oven on to 400°F (200°C). Cook the bacon in the frying pan over medium heat for 5 to 6 minutes until just starting to become crisp. Drain and discard most of the fat. Add the mushrooms and continue to stir until the mushrooms are soft, bacon is browned and liquid is evaporated. Remove from the heat to the hot pad.

2. Stir in the next 5 ingredients.

3. Spread the process cheese on each of the 12 bun halves. Top each with 2 tbsp. (30 mL) of the bacon mixture, spreading evenly. Cover the mixture with the cheese. Place on the ungreased baking sheet. Bake for 6 minutes until the cheese is bubbly. Use the oven mitts to remove the baking sheet to the wire rack. Makes 12 pizzas.

Pizza Pinwheels

Best served hot from the oven rather than reheating. Tangy and attractive.

Get It Together: baking sheet, dry measures, liquid measures, medium bowl, mixing spoon, rolling pin, ruler, measuring spoons, medium bowl, sharp knife, oven mitts, wire rack

1. Biscuit mix	2 1/4 cups	550 mL
Water	1/2 cup	125 mL
Biscuit mix, as needed, to prevent sticking when rolling		
2. Can of pizza (or tomato) sauce	7 1/2 oz.	213 mL
Green onions, sliced	2	2
Finely chopped green or red pepper	1/2 cup	125 mL
Finely chopped pepperoni (or other cooked sausage type of meat)	1/2 cup	125 mL
Grated mozzarella cheese	1 cup	250 mL
Dried oregano	1/4 tsp.	1 mL

1. Place the oven rack in the centre position. Turn the oven on to 400°F (200°C). Grease the baking sheet. Combine the biscuit mix and water in the medium bowl until it starts to form a ball. Turn the dough out onto the counter that has been lightly dusted with more biscuit mix. Gently knead the dough 20 times. Dust with biscuit mix and roll out to a 12 x 12 inch (30 x 30 cm) rectangle.

2. Combine the remaining 6 ingredients in the small bowl. Mix well. Spread over the dough, leaving about 1 inch (2.5 cm) all around the outside edge. Roll up the dough from 1 side to the other like a jelly roll. Pinch along the long edge of the roll to seal. Cut into twelve 1 inch (2.5 cm) thick slices. Place on the baking sheet. Bake in the oven for 12 minutes. Use the oven mitts to remove the baking sheet to the wire rack. Makes 12 little pizzas.

Pictured on page 71.

Build-Your-Pita Pizzas

These pizzas can be assembled and frozen before baking. When those hunger pangs hit, pop the frozen pizza in the oven and broil for eight to nine minutes.

Get It Together: measuring spoons, spreading knife, dry measures, baking sheet, oven mitts, wire rack

1. Pita breads (8 inch, 20 cm, size)   2   2
   Pizza sauce   3 tbsp.   45 mL

2. Any combination of the   2/3 cup   150 mL
   following toppings:
   chopped fresh mushrooms,
   chopped green pepper,
   chopped tomato, chopped
   green onion, pineapple
   tidbits, cooked crumbled
   bacon, deli meat (such as
   ham and pepperoni),
   to make

3. Grated mozzarella cheese   1/2 cup   125 mL

1. Place the oven rack in the centre position. Turn the oven on to broil. Spread each pita with 1 1/2 tbsp. (25 mL) of the sauce. Be sure to spread it right to the edges.

2. Sprinkle each pita with 1/2 of the toppings.

3. Sprinkle the toppings with the cheese. Lay the pitas on the ungreased baking sheet. Broil for 8 to 9 minutes until the cheese is melted and the edges are crispy. Use the oven mitts to remove the baking sheet to the wire rack. Makes 2 pita pizzas.

Pictured on page 90.

Did you know?

Be careful to prevent cutting your knuckles when grating cheese. Hold a large piece of cheese in one hand and the grater in the other hand. Press the cheese firmly into the holes on the grater as you move the cheese from top to bottom. Continue until you have the amount of cheese needed.

Individual Stuffed Pizzas

Golden semi-circles of pizza delights! Fresh bread flavour.

Get It Together: baking sheet, 1-3 medium bowls, dry measures, measuring spoons, large bowl, mixing spoons, liquid measures, table fork, tea towel, small saucepan, oven mitts, wire rack

1. PIZZA BASE

All-purpose flour	2 cups	500 mL
Salt	1/4 tsp.	1 mL
Grated Parmesan cheese	1 tbsp.	15 mL
Envelope of instant dry yeast (measure 1 1/2 tsp., 7 mL)	1/2 x 1/4 oz.	1/2 x 8 g
Hot water	3/4 cup	175 mL
Olive (or cooking) oil	1 tbsp.	15 mL

2. CHEESY CHICKEN FILLING

Chopped cooked chicken	1 cup	250 mL
Finely diced celery	1/4 cup	60 mL
Green onion, sliced	1	1
Grated mozzarella cheese	3/4 cup	175 mL
Dried basil	1/4 tsp.	1 mL
Garlic salt	1/4 tsp.	1 mL

3. PEPPERONI FILLING

Diced pepperoni	2/3 cup	150 mL
Pizza sauce	1/3 cup	75 mL
Finely diced green pepper	1/4 cup	60 mL
Grated carrot	1/4 cup	60 mL
Grated mozzarella cheese	3/4 cup	175 mL

4. VEGETABLE FILLING

Tub margarine	1 tbsp.	15 mL
All-purpose flour	1 tbsp.	15 mL
Milk	1/2 cup	125 mL
Bite-size pieces of cooked vegetables	1 1/2 cups	375 mL
Garlic salt	1/4 tsp.	1 mL
Pepper, sprinkle		
Grated mozzarella (or Cheddar) cheese	2/3 cup	150 mL
Grated Parmesan cheese	1 tbsp.	15 mL

(continued on the next page)

1. **Pizza Base:** Place the oven rack in the centre position. Turn the oven on to 400°F (200°C). Grease the baking sheet and 1 medium bowl. Stir the flour, salt, Parmesan cheese and yeast together in the large bowl. Add the water and oil. Stir into the dry mixture with the fork until most of the flour is mixed in. Turn the dough out onto the counter that has been lightly dusted with some flour. Using your hands, and sprinkling flour, as needed, to keep dough from sticking, knead the dough for about 3 minutes until smooth and stretchy. Place in the greased bowl. Cover with the tea towel and set aside for 45 minutes while filling is being made. When filling is ready, punch down and knead the dough to remove air pockets. Divide into 4 even portions. Roll into balls and press each ball out evenly on lightly greased counter into a 6 inch (15 cm) circle. Continue assembling by following the directions with 1 of the fillings of your choice below.

2. **Cheesy Chicken Filling:** Combine all 6 ingredients well in the medium bowl. Makes 1 2/3 cups (400 mL) filling. Place 6 tbsp. (100 mL) of the filling on each of the dough circles to 1 side of the centre. Fold the side without the filling over top of the filling and pinch the edges together well to seal. Place on the baking sheet. Bake in the oven for 20 minutes. Use the oven mitts to remove the pan to the wire rack. Makes 4 pizzas.

3. **Pepperoni Filling:** Combine all 5 ingredients well in the medium bowl. Makes 1 1/2 cups (375 mL) filling. Place 1/3 cup (75 mL) of the filling on each of the dough circles to 1 side of the centre. Fold the side without the filling over top of the filling and pinch the edges together well to seal. Place on the baking sheet. Bake in the oven for 20 minutes. Use the oven mitts to remove the pan to the wire rack. Makes 4 pizzas.

Pictured on page 126.

4. **Vegetable Filling:** Combine the margarine and flour in the small saucepan over medium heat. Add the milk, stirring until thickened. Stir in the 5 remaining ingredients, stirring until the cheese is melted and well combined. Cool. Makes 1 1/2 cups (375 mL) filling. Place 1/3 cup (75 mL) of the cooled filling on each of the dough circles to 1 side of the centre. Fold the side without the filling over top of the filling and pinch the edges together well to seal. Place on the baking sheet. Bake in the oven for 20 minutes. Use the oven mitts to remove the pan to the wire rack. Makes 4 pizzas.

Salsa Pizza

Salsa instead of pizza sauce—zippy!

Get It Together: baking sheet, measuring spoons, dry measures, oven mitts, wire rack

1. Pita bread (8 inch, 20 cm, size)	**1**	**1**
2. Chunky salsa (mild, medium or hot)	**2 tbsp.**	**30 mL**
Grated Cheddar or mozzarella cheese	**1/3 cup**	**75 mL**
Diced red or green pepper (optional)	**1/4 cup**	**60 mL**

1. Place the oven rack in the centre position. Turn the oven on to 400°F (200°C). Place the pita bread on the ungreased baking sheet. Flatten with your hand.

2. Spread the salsa on the pita bread using the back of the measuring spoon. Sprinkle with the cheese. Add the peppers. Bake in the oven for about 10 minutes or until the cheese is melted and the edge of the pita is crisp. Use the oven mitts to remove the baking sheet to the wire rack. Let stand 2 minutes before cutting. Cuts into 6 wedges.

Pictured on page 89.

1. Pita Pizza Classic, page 94
2. Salsa Pizza, above

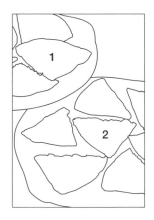

Tortilla Pizzas

Wedges are easy to hold in your hands to eat.

Get It Together: baking sheet, dry measures, table spoon, measuring spoons, oven mitts, wire rack, sharp knife

1.

White (or whole-wheat) flour tortillas (10 inch, 25 cm, size)	2	2
Pizza sauce	1/4 cup	60 mL

2.

Finely chopped green pepper	1/4 cup	60 mL
Finely chopped mushrooms	1/4 cup	60 mL
Grated mozzarella cheese	1 cup	250 mL
Dried oregano	1 tsp.	5 mL

1. Place the oven rack in the centre position. Turn the oven on to 375°F (190°C). Lay the 2 tortillas on the ungreased baking sheet. Spread 2 tbsp. (30 mL) of the pizza sauce on each of the tortillas, using the back of the spoon, spreading sauce almost to the edges.

2. Divide and sprinkle the green pepper, mushrooms, cheese and oregano evenly over one half of each of the tortillas. Fold side without the filling over top of the filling to make a half-moon shape. Bake in the oven for 15 minutes until crisp and golden. Use the oven mitts to remove the baking sheet to the wire rack. Let stand for 5 minutes. Cut into wedges to serve. Makes 2 individual pizzas.

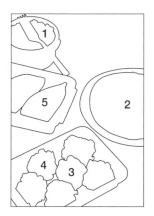

1. Macaroni & Cottage Cheese, page 63
2. Build-Your-Pita Pizzas, page 85
3. Peanut Butter Popcorn Treats, page 131
4. Choco-Peanut Butter Popcorn Balls, page 131
5. Pickly Pita Pockets, page 120

Pizza Sticks

Slightly crusty golden strips of bread. Specks of sausage throughout. Nippy taste.

Get It Together: baking sheet, dry measures, measuring spoons, large bowl, mixing spoons, liquid measures, rolling pin, ruler, sharp knife, tea towel, small cup, pastry brush, oven mitts, wire rack, small saucepan

1. **STICKS**

All-purpose flour	2 cups	500 mL
Salt	1/2 tsp.	2 mL
Granulated sugar	1/4 tsp.	1 mL
Dried basil	1/2 tsp.	2 mL
Envelope of instant dry yeast (1 scant tbsp., 15 mL)	1 x 1/4 oz.	1 x 8 g
Olive (or cooking) oil	1 1/2 tbsp.	25 mL
Hot water	1 cup	250 mL
All-purpose flour, approximately	1/2 cup	125 mL
Chopped pepperoni	2/3 cup	150 mL

2.

Hard margarine, melted	2 tbsp.	30 mL
Garlic powder	1/4 tsp.	1 mL

3. **DIPPING SAUCE**

Can of tomato sauce	7 1/2 oz.	213 mL
Garlic salt	1/4 tsp.	1 mL
Onion powder	1/4 tsp.	1 mL
Dried oregano	1/2 tsp.	2 mL
Ketchup	2 tbsp.	30 mL
Granulated sugar, just a pinch		

(continued on the next page)

1. **Sticks:** Place the oven rack in the centre position. Grease the baking sheet. Stir the first 5 ingredients together in the bowl. Pour in the olive oil and hot water and stir together until the flour is combined. Work in the second amount of flour until no longer sticky. Turn out onto lightly floured surface. Knead for about 5 minutes, adding more flour as needed and a bit of the chopped pepperoni as you do, until all the pepperoni is mixed into the dough. Invert the bowl over the dough. Let the dough rest for 10 minutes. Roll the dough out to about 1/2 inch (12 mm) thick. Using the knife, cut rows about 1 inch (2.5 cm) wide and then cut crosswise into 5 inch (12.5 cm) sticks. Lay each stick on the baking sheet, about 2 inches (5 cm) apart. Cover with the tea towel. Let rise in the oven, with the door closed and the oven light on, for 30 minutes. Remove the baking sheet from the oven. Turn the oven on to 375°F (190°C).

2. Combine the melted margarine and garlic powder in the cup. Brush the sticks with the margarine mixture. Bake in the oven for 20 minutes. Use the oven mitts to remove the baking sheet to the wire rack. Makes 18 to 20 sticks.

3. **Dipping Sauce:** Combine all 6 ingredients in the small saucepan. Bring mixture to a simmer over low heat. Simmer for 15 minutes, stirring occasionally. Use as a dip for the pizza sticks. Makes 3/4 cup (175 mL).

Pictured on page 143.

Pita Pizza Classic

If you like a thin-crust pizza, this is the one for you.

Get It Together: baking sheet, measuring spoons, dry measures, oven mitts, wire rack

1. Pita bread (8 inch, 20 cm, size)	1	1
2. Pizza or spaghetti sauce	2 tbsp.	30 mL
3. Chopped cooked meat (ham, pepperoni, bacon or sausage)	2 tbsp.	30 mL
Fresh mushrooms, chopped	2	2
Grated mozzarella cheese	1/3 cup	75 mL
Diced green pepper	2 tbsp.	30 mL

1. Place the oven rack in the top position. Turn the oven on to broil. Place the pita bread on the ungreased baking sheet. Flatten with your hand.

2. Spread the pizza sauce over the pita almost to the edges using the back of the measuring spoon.

3. Sprinkle the ham, mushrooms, cheese and green pepper over the sauce. Broil on the top rack in the oven for about 7 minutes or until the cheese is melted and the edge of the pita is crisp. Use the oven mitts to remove the baking sheet to the wire rack to cool. Cuts into 6 wedges.

Pictured on page 89.

Tortellini Salad

A colourful and tasty salad.

Get It Together: liquid measures, measuring spoons, large saucepan, dry measures, colander, medium bowl, mixing spoon, plastic wrap

1.

Water	6 cups	1.5 L
Salt	1 tsp.	5 mL
Fresh (or dried) cheese-filled tortellini	1 cup	250 mL

2.

Diced English cucumber, with peel	1/2 cup	125 mL
Small tomato, diced	1	1
Thinly sliced green onion	1/4 cup	60 mL
Thinly slivered green or red pepper	1/2 cup	125 mL
Salt	1/2 tsp.	2 mL
Pepper	1/8 tsp.	0.5 mL

1. Bring the water and first amount of salt to a boil in the saucepan. Add the tortellini and cook for about 10 minutes until tender but still firm. Drain in the colander. Rinse with cold water until cool. Drain well.

2. Combine the pasta with the remaining 6 ingredients in the bowl. Stir well. Cover with plastic wrap. Chill in the refrigerator for 30 minutes to blend the flavours. Makes 3 1/2 cups (875 mL).

Pictured on page 18.

Potato Salad

Dill pickles add a great flavour to this creamy salad.

Get It Together: sharp knife, cutting board, liquid measures, measuring spoons, small saucepan, medium bowl, mixing spoon, dry measures, small cup, plastic wrap

1.
Medium potatoes, peeled	2	2
Water	2 cups	500 mL
Salt	1/4 tsp.	1 mL

2.
Large hard-boiled eggs, chopped	2	2
Celery rib, thinly sliced	1	1
Small dill pickles, chopped and blotted dry with paper towel	3	3

3.
Mayonnaise (or salad dressing)	1/4 cup	60 mL
Italian (or other non-creamy) dressing	2 tbsp.	30 mL
Salt, sprinkle (optional)		
Pepper, sprinkle (optional)		

1. Cut each of the potatoes into 4 pieces on the cutting board. Place the potato, water and first amount of salt in the saucepan. Cover. Bring to a boil over medium heat. Boil for about 15 minutes until tender. Drain. Place in the bowl to cool.

2. Add the egg, celery and pickles to the potato. Stir well.

3. Combine the mayonnaise and Italian dressing in the cup. Stir into the potato mixture. Sprinkle with salt and pepper. Stir. Cover with plastic wrap. Chill in the refrigerator for at least 30 minutes. Makes 2 3/4 cups (675 mL).

Did you know?

To peel a hard boiled egg, tap it on the kitchen counter to crack the shell. Roll it between your hands to loosen the shell. Hold it under cold water as you peel it.

Marinated Vegetables

This salad will keep for one week in the refrigerator. The flavour just keeps getting better.

Get It Together: dry measures, medium microwave-safe bowl with lid (or plastic wrap), measuring spoons, microwave oven, oven mitts, hot pad, large bowl, mixing spoon, liquid measures

1.	Broccoli florets	2 cups	500 mL
	Cauliflower florets	2 cups	500 mL
	Water	1 tbsp.	15 mL
2.	Thinly sliced carrot	1 cup	250 mL
	Sliced celery	1/2 cup	125 mL
	Green onion, sliced	1	1
	Medium red or yellow pepper, sliced	1	1
	Diced English cucumber, with peel	1 cup	250 mL
3.	Italian (or other non-creamy) dressing	1/2 cup	125 mL

1. Combine the broccoli and cauliflower in the bowl. Sprinkle with the water. Cover the bowl, leaving a small opening for the steam to escape. Microwave on high (100%) for 2 minutes. Use the oven mitts to remove the bowl to the hot pad. Let stand, covered, for 2 minutes.

2. Place the next 5 ingredients in the large bowl. Add the broccoli and cauliflower. Stir.

3. Pour the dressing over the vegetables. Stir well. Chill in the refrigerator until cold. Makes 8 cups (2 L).

Rice Salad

This salad can also be stuffed into a pita bread for a salad sandwich.

Get It Together: dry measures, measuring spoons, small bowl, mixing spoon

1. | | | |
|---|---|---|
| Cooked rice | 3/4 cup | 175 mL |
| Cooked ham, chopped | 2 oz. | 57 g |
| Sliced green onion | 2 tbsp. | 30 mL |
| Cooked vegetables (such as peas, broccoli florets or green beans) | 1/2 cup | 125 mL |
| Grated carrot | 1/4 cup | 60 mL |
| Olive oil | 1 tsp. | 5 mL |
| White (or wine or cider) vinegar | 2 tsp. | 10 mL |
| Salt, sprinkle | | |

1. Combine all 8 ingredients in the bowl. Mix well. Makes 1 1/2 cups (375 mL).

Pictured on page 72.

Variation: Add 2 tbsp. (30 mL) of sunflower seeds or pumpkin seeds, or add 1/4 cup (60 mL) of raisins.

Cucumber & Pea Salad

You can make this salad the night before to take to school the next day. A crunchy, refreshing salad.

Get It Together: dry measures, measuring spoons, small bowl, mixing spoon, small cup, table spoon

1. | | | |
|---|---|---|
| Diced English cucumber, with peel | 1 cup | 250 mL |
| Frozen baby peas, thawed | 1/2 cup | 125 mL |
| Sliced green onion | 2 tbsp. | 30 mL |
| Garlic salt, sprinkle | | |
| Pepper, sprinkle | | |
| Cubed Cheddar (or Swiss) cheese (1/2 inch, 12 mm, size) | 1/2 cup | 125 mL |

(continued on the next page)

2. DRESSING

Mayonnaise (or salad dressing)	2 tbsp.	30 mL
Granulated sugar	2 tsp.	10 mL
Lemon juice	1 tsp.	5 mL

1. Combine the first 6 ingredients in the bowl. Stir well.

2. **Dressing:** Mix the mayonnaise, sugar and lemon juice in the cup. Add to the vegetable mixture. Mix well. Makes 2 cups (500 mL).

Pictured on page 108.

Tomato & Mozza Salad

This salad tastes even better when left to stand awhile. Great to take for lunch.

Get It Together: sharp knife, cutting board, paper towel, small bowl, measuring spoons, mixing spoon, dry measures

1. Medium tomatoes	2	2
2. Olive oil	2 tsp.	10 mL
Garlic salt	1/4 tsp.	1 mL
Pepper, sprinkle		
Dried basil	1/4 tsp.	1 mL
Sliced green onion	1 tbsp.	15 mL
Black olives, sliced (optional)	4	4
3. Grated mozzarella cheese	1/2 cup	125 mL

1. Cut the tomato in half on the cutting board. Gently squeeze the tomato halves over the paper towel to remove the seeds. Discard the seeds and juice. Dice the tomato into bite-size pieces. Place in the bowl.

2. Add the next 6 ingredients. Stir.

3. Stir in the cheese. Makes 1 1/2 cups (375 mL).

Pictured on page 107.

Variation: Spoon salad onto baguette slices. Place slices on a baking sheet. Broil on the top rack in the oven until the cheese is melted.

Lemon Sauced Fruit

Chunks of fruit in a colourful syrup. Can be a fruit salad or a dessert.

Get It Together: medium bowl, mixing spoon, liquid measures, small bowl, whisk, covered container

1. | | | |
   |---|---|---|
   | Canned fruit cocktail, drained, juice reserved | 14 oz. | 398 mL |
   | Canned mandarin orange segments, drained, juice reserved | 10 oz. | 284 mL |
   | Medium bananas, diced | 2 | 2 |

2. | | | |
   |---|---|---|
   | Reserved fruit cocktail and mandarin orange juice, plus pineapple, apple or orange juice, to make | 1 1/2 cups | 375 mL |
   | Instant lemon pudding powder, 4 serving size | 1 | 1 |

1. Combine the fruit cocktail, oranges and banana in the medium bowl. Stir.

2. Combine the reserved juices and pudding powder in the small bowl. Whisk for 2 minutes. Fold into the fruit. Store any remaining salad in the container in the refrigerator for up to 5 days. Makes 4 cups (1 L).

Bean & Tomato Salad

A delicious crunchy salad. Perfect to take to school for lunch.

Get It Together: dry measures, medium bowl, mixing spoon, measuring spoons, small bowl, plastic wrap, covered container

1. | | | |
   |---|---|---|
   | Canned chickpeas (garbanzo beans), drained and rinsed | 19 oz. | 540 mL |
   | Thinly sliced celery | 1/2 cup | 125 mL |
   | Green onion, thinly sliced | 1 | 1 |
   | Diced red pepper | 1/2 cup | 125 mL |
   | Canned stewed tomatoes, drained and chopped | 14 oz. | 398 mL |

(continued on the next page)

2. DRESSING

Olive (or vegetable) oil	2 tbsp.	30 mL
White vinegar	2 tbsp.	30 mL
Dried basil	1/2 tsp.	2 mL
Dry mustard	1/4 tsp.	1 mL
Garlic powder	1/8 tsp.	0.5 mL
Parsley flakes	2 tsp.	10 mL

1. Combine the first 5 ingredients in the medium bowl. Stir well.

2. **Dressing:** Combine the remaining 6 ingredients in the small bowl. Pour over the vegetable mixture. Mix well. Cover with plastic wrap. Marinate in the refrigerator for several hours or overnight, stirring several times. Store any remaining salad in the container in the refrigerator for up to 3 days. Makes 4 cups (1 L).

Pictured on page 53 and on back cover.

Cottage Cheese Salad

Very colourful. A great blend of flavours.

Get It Together: dry measures, measuring spoons, small bowl, mixing spoon, covered container

1. Cottage cheese	1 cup	250 mL
Diced English cucumber, with peel	1/4 cup	60 mL
Grated carrot	2 tbsp.	30 mL
Diced red pepper	2 tbsp.	30 mL
Garlic salt	1/8 tsp.	0.5 mL
Pepper, sprinkle		
Celery seed, sprinkle		

1. Combine all 7 ingredients in the bowl. Stir. Let the salad stand for 10 minutes to blend the flavours. Store any remaining salad in the container in the refrigerator for up to 24 hours. Makes 1 1/2 cups (375 mL).

Pictured on page 36.

Crunchy Potato Salad

Very colourful. Watch the cooking time of the potato. It will differ according to the size of your potato.

Get It Together: sharp knife, cutting board, liquid measures, measuring spoons, small saucepan, colander, medium bowl, mixing spoon, plastic wrap

1.			
Large potato, peeled	1	1
Water	1 cup	250 mL
Salt	1/4 tsp.	1 mL

2.			
Diced red pepper	2 tbsp.	30 mL
Grated carrot	1 tbsp.	15 mL
Finely diced celery	1 tbsp.	15 mL
Sliced green onion	1 tbsp.	15 mL
Grated Cheddar cheese	2 tbsp.	30 mL
Italian dressing	2 tbsp.	30 mL
Salt, sprinkle		
Pepper, sprinkle		

1. Cut the potato crosswise into 3 pieces on the cutting board. Put the potato pieces, water and first amount of salt into the saucepan. Bring to a boil. Reduce the heat to low. Cover. Simmer for about 13 minutes until the potato is tender when poked with the knife. Do not overcook or else the potato will be mushy. Drain in the colander. Cool slightly. Dice into small cubes on the cutting board.

2. Combine the potato and the remaining 8 ingredients in the bowl. Stir. Cover with plastic wrap. Chill in the refrigerator until cold. Makes 1 1/2 cups (375 mL).

Pictured on page 17.

Did you know?

You can use a thermos to bring your salad for lunch. Chill a wide-mouth thermos with ice water and let stand for 5 minutes. Drain thermos and fill with thoroughly chilled salad.

Peas 'N' Pasta Salad

Best eaten the same day. If you would like to save half of this salad to take in your lunch tomorrow, simply pour 3 tbsp. (50 mL) of the dressing now, and save 3 tbsp. (45 mL) to pour over the salad before you go to school.

Get It Together: liquid measures, large saucepan, measuring spoons, dry measures, mixing spoon, colander, medium bowl, sharp knife, cutting board, paper towel, liquid measures

1.

Water	6 cups	1.5 L
Salt	1 tsp.	5 mL
Cooking oil (optional)	1 tsp.	5 mL
Fusilli (or rotini) pasta	1 cup	250 mL
Frozen baby peas	1/2 cup	125 mL

2.

Sliced green onion	2 tbsp.	30 mL
Grated carrot	2 tbsp.	30 mL
Small tomato	1	1
Cubed Cheddar (or other firm) cheese (1/2 inch, 12 mm, size)	1/2 cup	125 mL
Italian (or other non-creamy) dressing	1/3 cup	75 mL

1. Bring the water in the saucepan to a boil over high heat. Add the salt and cooking oil. Add the fusilli. When the water returns to a boil, reduce the heat to medium-high. Cook the pasta for 8 minutes, stirring occasionally. Add the peas to the pasta and water. Cook for 1 minute until the pasta is tender but still firm. Drain in the colander. Run cold water over. Drain well.

2. Combine the green onion and carrot in the bowl. Add the pasta and peas. Cut the tomato in half on the cutting board. Gently squeeze the tomato halves over the paper towel to remove the seeds. Discard the seeds and juice. Dice the tomato into 1/2 inch (12 mm) chunks. Add to the bowl. Add the cheese. Stir in the dressing just before serving. Makes 3 1/2 cups (875 mL).

Pictured on the front cover.

Apple Burgers

Try topping the patty with applesauce instead of mustard and ketchup.

Get It Together: dry measures, measuring spoons, medium bowl, mixing spoon, broiler pan, oven mitts, wire rack, pancake lifter

1.

Lean ground chicken (or turkey)	1 lb.	454 g
Applesauce, page 22	1/2 cup	125 mL
Finely chopped onion	2 tbsp.	30 mL
Finely chopped green or red pepper	2 tbsp.	30 mL
Seasoning salt	3/4 tsp.	4 mL
Pepper	1/8 tsp.	0.5 mL

2.

Hamburger buns, split in half (fresh or toasted)	6	6

1. Place the oven rack in the top position. Turn the oven on to broil. Mix all 6 ingredients in the bowl. Divide the mixture into 6 portions. Form each portion into a patty. Place on the ungreased broiler pan. Broil in the oven for 8 minutes. Use the oven mitts to remove the broiler pan to the wire rack. Flip the patties over with the pancake lifter. Broil for 8 minutes until patties are lightly browned and no longer pink inside.

2. Place 1 patty on the bottom half of each bun. Cover with the top halves of the buns. Makes 6 burgers.

Did you know?
When using a liquid measure, place it on a level counter. Bend down and watch as you fill it. Fill only to the line marking the amount called for in the recipe. Liquid measures shouldn't be used for ingredients such as flour or margarine because they cannot be levelled accurately.

Chick 'N' Cheese Burgers

Burgers may be made ahead and frozen individually. Simply place frozen burger in your lunch bag in the morning and microwave on high (100%) for one minute to heat at lunchtime.

Get It Together: measuring spoons, frying pan, mixing spoon, liquid measures, dry measures

1. Cooking oil	1 tsp.	5 mL
Lean ground chicken	1 lb.	454 g
Medium onion, chopped	1	1
Celery rib, chopped	1	1
2. All-purpose flour	3 tbsp.	50 mL
Salt	1/2 tsp.	2 mL
Pepper	1/4 tsp.	1 mL
Garlic powder, just a pinch (optional)		
Milk	3/4 cup	175 mL
3. Grated Cheddar cheese	1 1/2 cups	375 mL
Process Cheddar cheese slices, broken up	2	2
Prepared mustard	2 tsp.	10 mL
4. Hamburger buns, cut in half	6	6

1. Heat the cooking oil in the frying pan over medium heat. Scramble-fry the chicken, onion and celery in the oil until the chicken is no longer pink and the vegetables are tender-crisp.

2. Sprinkle with the flour, salt, pepper and garlic powder. Stir for 1 minute. Stir in the milk gradually until bubbling and thickened.

3. Add the next 3 ingredients. Stir until the cheese is melted. Makes 3 1/3 cups (825 mL).

4. Pull out bits of bread from the soft centre of the top and bottom halves of the buns, making a shallow hollow. Fill each of the 6 bottom halves with a heaping 1/2 cup (125 mL) of the chicken mixture. Cover with the top halves of the buns. Makes 6 burgers.

Pepper Cheese Roll

Coloured peppers make this a real treat. This can be made ahead and wrapped with plastic wrap and refrigerated for up to two days.

Get It Together: bread knife, cutting board, measuring spoons, pastry brush, dry measures

1.
Whole-wheat roll, oblong (or oval) shape (about 5 inches, 12.5 cm, long)	1	1
Italian dressing	1 tbsp.	15 mL
Red, orange or yellow pepper, cut into thin strips	1/2	1/2
Pepper, sprinkle		
Dried basil, just a pinch		
White cheese (such as mozzarella, Swiss or Monterey Jack), thinly sliced	2 oz.	57 g
Alfalfa (or mixed) sprouts (optional)	1/4 cup	60 mL

1. Cut the roll in half horizontally on the cutting board. Remove a bit of bread from the soft centre of the top and bottom halves, making a slight hollow. Brush the dressing onto each half of the roll. Layer the pepper strips lengthwise across the bottom half. Sprinkle with pepper and basil. Lay the cheese slices over top. Cover with the sprouts. Lay the top half of the roll over the sprouts. Makes 1 sandwich.

Pictured on page 36.

1. Tomato & Mozza Salad, page 99
2. Hawaiian Grilled Cheese, page 115
3. Peanut Butter & Pickle Sandwich, 114
4. Snap Gingers, page 29
5. Ham & Cuke Sandwich, page 116

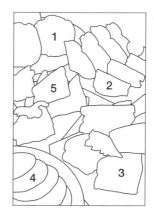

Peanut Butter & Bacon Sandwich

Make this sandwich and wrap it with plastic wrap and take it to school. Heat in the microwave oven when ready for lunch.

Get It Together: frying pan, tongs, paper towel, measuring spoons, table knife

1. **Bacon slices (see Note)**	2	2
2. **Peanut butter**	1 1/2 tbsp.	25 mL
White (or whole-wheat)	2	2
bread slices, toasted		
Process Mozzarella cheese slice	1	1
Tub margarine	1 1/2 tsp.	7 mL

1. Cook the bacon in the frying pan over medium heat until crisp. Use the tongs to turn the bacon. Remove the bacon to the paper towel, blotting well.

2. Spread the peanut butter on 1 slice of toast. Break each slice of bacon into 2 pieces. Lay all 4 pieces over the peanut butter. Top with the cheese slice. Spread the other slice of toast with the margarine. Place, buttered side down, over the cheese. Makes 1 sandwich.

Note: Bacon may be cooked in the microwave oven instead of a frying pan. Simply place the bacon between paper towels and microwave on high (100%) for 3 minutes until crisp. Remove to a clean paper towel and blot well to remove the fat.

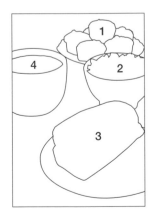

1. Gingerbran Cream Muffins, page 28
2. Cucumber & Pea Salad, page 98
3. Super Sausage Subs, page 113
4. Corn Chowder, page 134

Egg Roll Buns

These take a little extra time, but they are worth it! Make them ahead and refrigerate or freeze. Reheat for your lunch.

Get It Together: non-stick frying pan, mixing spoon, dry measures, measuring spoons, baking sheet, table spoon, pastry brush, oven mitts, wire rack

1. Lean ground chicken	1/2 lb.	225 g
Grated carrot	1/4 cup	60 mL
Finely chopped celery	1/4 cup	60 mL
Bean sprouts, chopped	1/2 cup	125 mL
Chopped fresh mushrooms	1/4 cup	60 mL
2. Garlic powder	1/8 tsp.	0.5 mL
Pepper, sprinkle		
Green onion, thinly sliced	1	1
Black bean (or oyster) sauce	2 tbsp.	30 mL
3. Tube of refrigerator country-style biscuits (10 biscuits per tube)	12 oz.	340 g
4. Large egg, fork-beaten	1	1
Sesame seeds	1 tbsp.	15 mL

1. Scramble-fry the ground chicken in the frying pan over medium heat for 3 minutes. Add the carrot and celery. Scramble-fry for 3 to 5 minutes. Add the bean sprouts and mushrooms. Cook until the liquid is gone.

2. Stir in the next 4 ingredients. Cook for about 2 minutes. Remove from the heat to cool. Makes 2 cups (500 mL).

3. Place the oven rack in the centre position. Turn the oven on to 375°F (190°C). Grease the baking sheet. Open the biscuits and separate each and flatten into a 4 inch (10 cm) circle. Divide the filling evenly among the centre of each circle. Bring the edges up and pinch together well to seal. Place seam side down on the baking sheet.

4. Using the pastry brush, brush the tops of each bun with the egg. Sprinkle with the sesame seeds. Bake in the oven for 15 to 16 minutes until golden. Use the oven mitts to remove the baking sheet to the wire rack. Makes 10 buns.

Pictured on page 36.

Tuna Buns

Great warm or cold.

Get It Together: measuring spoons, dry measures, medium bowl, mixing spoon, frying pan, pancake lifter, table knife

1.

Canned flaked tuna in water, with liquid	6 1/2 oz.	184 g
Large egg, fork-beaten	1	1
Minced onion flakes	1 tsp.	5 mL
Small carrot, grated	1	1
Fine dry bread crumbs	1/2 cup	125 mL
Parsley flakes	1 tsp.	5 mL
Lemon juice	1 tsp.	5 mL
Salt, sprinkle		
Pepper, sprinkle		

2.

Cooking oil	1 tsp.	5 mL

3.

Mayonnaise (or salad dressing)	2 tbsp.	30 mL
Kaiser buns, split	4	4
Lettuce leaves	4	4

1. Combine the first 9 ingredients in the bowl. Mix well. Form into 4 patties.

2. Heat the cooking oil in the frying pan over medium heat. Cook the patties for about 2 minutes until golden brown. Turn the patties over with the pancake lifter to cook the other side. Cook for 2 minutes until golden brown and crispy.

3. Spread the mayonnaise on the bottom of each bun. Place 1 patty on top of mayonnaise. Top with lettuce. Cover with the top halves of the buns. Makes 4 buns.

Pictured on page 17.

Barbecue Beef Buns

Great warm or cold. These freeze well. Simply take from the freezer and put it in your lunch bag. At lunchtime, warm in the microwave on high (100%) for one minute.

Get It Together: non-stick frying pan, mixing spoon, measuring spoons, liquid measures, baking sheet, oven mitts, wire rack

1.	Lean ground beef	1/2 lb.	225 g
	Small onion, cut into rings	1	1
2.	Seasoning salt	1/2 tsp.	2 mL
	Paprika	1/2 tsp.	2 mL
	Regular (or smoky-flavoured) barbecue sauce	1/2 cup	125 mL
3.	Tube of refrigerator crescent rolls (8 rolls per tube)	8 1/2 oz.	235 g

1. Place the oven rack in the centre position. Turn the oven on to 375°F (190°C). Scramble-fry the ground beef in the frying pan over medium heat until almost brown. Add the onion rings. Scramble-fry for 2 minutes until the ground beef is no longer pink and the onion is soft.

2. Stir in the salt and paprika. Add the barbecue sauce. Simmer, uncovered, for 10 minutes until the liquid is gone. Cool.

3. Open the crescent rolls and separate into 8 triangles. Place 2 tbsp. (30 mL) of the beef mixture on each triangle. Bring the 3 points of each triangle to the centre over the meat and pinch all of the edges together well to seal. Form into round shapes. Place each ball, seam side down on the ungreased baking sheet. Bake in the oven for 12 to 15 minutes until golden. Use the oven mitts to remove the baking sheet to the wire rack. Makes 8 buns.

Did you know?

Cook food in the microwave oven for the minimum time stated in the recipe. If more cooking time is required, add only 30 seconds at a time. It's better to add more time and cook the food just right rather than overcook the food.

Super Sausage Subs

These will freeze well. Simply thaw before heating or pop in your lunch bag in the morning and by noon, the sub is well thawed. Heat in the microwave for one minute. A great lunch!

Get It Together: non-stick frying pan, mixing spoon, measuring spoons, liquid measures, dry measures

1.

Ground sausage meat	1 lb.	454 g
Medium green pepper, cut into slivers	1	1
Medium onion, sliced	1	1
Pepper	1/8 tsp.	0.5 mL
Paprika	1/2 tsp.	2 mL
Cayenne pepper, sprinkle		
Meatless pasta sauce	1 cup	250 mL

2.

Submarine buns (10 inches, 25 cm, long), cut in half horizontally	4	4
Grated Cheddar (or mozzarella) cheese	1 cup	250 mL

1. Scramble-fry the sausage in the frying pan over medium heat for 10 minutes, breaking up any large lumps as it cooks. Drain. Add the green pepper, onion, pepper, paprika and cayenne pepper. Scramble-fry for 10 minutes until the vegetables are tender-crisp and the sausage is no longer pink. Stir in the pasta sauce. Remove from the heat. Makes 3 cups (750 mL).

2. Pull out bits of bread from the soft centre of the top and bottom halves of the buns, making a shallow hollow. Divide the sausage mixture among the 4 bottom bun halves. Top each with 1/4 cup (60 mL) of the cheese. Lay the top bun halves over the filling to make a sandwich. Ready to eat. Makes 4 sandwiches.

Pictured on page 108.

Variation: These can be heated in the microwave oven on medium (50%) for 1 minute or wrapped with foil and heated in a 300°F (150°C) oven for 15 minutes.

The "New" Peanut Butter Sandwich

Alfalfa sprouts give peanut butter sandwiches a new kick! Great to wash down with a big glass of milk.

Get It Together: measuring spoons, table knife, dry measures, bread knife, cutting board

1.			
Peanut butter	2 tbsp.	30 mL
White (or whole-wheat) bagel, cut in half (toasted or fresh)	1	1
Jam (your favourite flavour)	2 tsp.	10 mL
Liquid honey	1 tsp.	5 mL
Packed alfalfa sprouts	1/2 cup	125 mL

1. Spread the peanut butter on each bagel half. Spread 1 of the bagel halves with jam and honey. Top with the sprouts. Press both bagel halves together. Cut in half on the cutting board. Makes 1 sandwich.

Peanut Butter & Pickle Sandwich

Who would have thought! Sounds interesting—but very tasty!

Get It Together: measuring spoons, table knife, paper towel, bread knife, cutting board

1.			
Peanut butter	2 tbsp.	30 mL
White (or whole-wheat) bread slices	2	2
2. Dill pickles, cut in half lengthwise	1-2	1-2

1. Spread the peanut butter on 1 side of each bread slice.

2. Lay the pickle on the paper towel for 1 to 2 minutes to soak up the juice. Lay the pickle slices on top of the peanut butter. Place second slice of bread on top, peanut butter side down. Cut in half on the cutting board. Makes 1 sandwich.

Variation: Spread peanut butter on a flour tortilla. Lay a small whole dill pickle on top of the tortilla at 1 end. Roll the tortilla around the pickle.

Pictured on page 107.

Grilled Raisin & Cheese

Raisin bread adds lots of flavour to this classic!

Get It Together: non-stick frying pan, table knife, pancake lifter, bread knife, cutting board

1. Tub margarine, for spreading
   Raisin bread slices   2   2
   Process cheese slices (or your
      favourite cheese), to cover

1. Heat the frying pan over medium-low heat. Spread the margarine on 1 side of each bread slice. Cover the unbuttered side of 1 slice of bread with the cheese. Lay the second slice of bread, buttered side up, on top of the cheese. Place the sandwich in the frying pan. When the bottom side is browned, flip the sandwich over to brown the other side. Cut in half on the cutting board. Makes 1 sandwich.

Hawaiian Grilled Cheese

The next best thing to visiting Hawaii.

Get It Together: non-stick frying pan, table knife, pancake lifter, bread knife, cutting board

1. Tub margarine, for spreading
   White (or whole-wheat)   2   2
      bread slices
   Thin process cheese slices   2   2
   Ham slice (1 oz., 28 g)   1   1
   Pineapple slices, blotted very   1-2   1-2
      dry with paper towel

1. Heat the frying pan over medium-low heat. Spread the margarine on 1 side of each bread slice. Place 1 slice of cheese on the unbuttered side of 1 slice. Place the ham, pineapple and remaining slice of cheese over top. Lay the second slice of bread, buttered side up, on top of the cheese. Place the sandwich in the frying pan. When the bottom side is browned, flip the sandwich over to brown the other side. Cut in half on the cutting board. Makes 1 sandwich.

Pictured on page 107.

Ham & Cuke Sandwich

Yummy to eat for lunch any day of the week.

Get It Together: measuring spoons, small bowl, mixing spoon, table knife, bread knife, cutting board

1.	Mayonnaise (or salad dressing)	2 tsp.	10 mL
	French (or Russian) dressing	2 tsp.	10 mL
	Whole-wheat (or white) bread slices	2	2
2.	Shaved ham slices (about 2 oz., 57 g)	2	2
	English cucumber slices, with peel	3-4	3-4

1. Combine the mayonnaise and French dressing in the bowl. Mix well. Spread mixture on both slices of bread.

2. Place the ham slices on 1 slice of bread. Top with the cucumber slices. Place the second slice of bread on top. Cut in half on the cutting board. Makes 1 sandwich.

Pictured on page 107.

Muffuletta

Pronounced muhf-ful-LEHT-tuh. Make this New Orleans sandwich the night before to take for lunch the next day.

Get It Together: measuring spoons, small cup, pastry brush, dry measures

1.	Italian-style crusty bun, cut in half horizontally	1	1
	Italian dressing	1 1/2 tbsp.	25 mL
	Tomato slices	4	4
	Mozzarella cheese slices	2	2
	Lean ham (or beef) slices (about 2 oz., 57 g)	2	2
	Alfalfa sprouts (or shredded lettuce)	1/3 cup	75 mL

(continued on the next page)

1. Pull out bits of bread from the soft centre of both bun halves. Put the dressing into the cup. Use the pastry brush to spread about 1/2 tbsp. (7 mL) of dressing on each half. Layer 2 slices of tomato, 1 slice of cheese and 1 slice of ham on the bottom half of the bun. Brush the remaining dressing over the ham. Top with the sprouts, remaining ham slice, remaining cheese slice and remaining tomato slices. Cover with the top half of the bun. Press the sandwich lightly together. Makes 1 sandwich.

Hero Sandwich

You will be a hero if you can finish this! You will be an even bigger hero if you share!

Get It Together: bread knife, cutting board, measuring spoons, table knife

1. **Submarine bun (12 inches,** **30 cm, long)**	1	1
Mayonnaise (or salad dressing)	1 tbsp.	15 mL
Prepared mustard	2 tsp.	10 mL
2. **Thin slices of salami (about** **1 1/2 oz., 43 g)**	6	6
Thinly shaved deli ham **(or chicken or turkey)**	1 1/2 oz.	43 g
Tomato slices	5	5
Mozzarella (or Monterey Jack) **cheese, thinly sliced**	2 oz.	57 g
Shredded lettuce (or mixed sprouts)	1/2 cup	125 mL
Salt, sprinkle		
Pepper, sprinkle		

1. Cut the submarine bun in half horizontally on the cutting board. Pull out bits of bread from the soft centre of the top and bottom halves, making a shallow hollow. Spread the mayonnaise on each half. Spread the mustard on the bottom half.

2. Layer the next 4 ingredients on top of the mustard-topped half. Top with the lettuce. Sprinkle with salt and pepper. Place the top half onto the filled bottom half. Press down slightly. Cut in half on the cutting board. Makes 1 sandwich.

Pictured on the front cover.

Toast Cups

Fill these with any sandwich filling.

Get It Together: dry measures, table knife, muffin pan (for 12 muffins), oven mitts, wire rack

1. **White (or whole-wheat)** **bread slices, crusts removed**	12	12
Tub margarine	1/3 cup	75 mL

1. Place the oven rack in the centre position. Turn the oven on to 350°F (175°C). Thinly spread 1 side of each bread slice with the margarine. Press each slice, buttered side down, into each ungreased muffin cup. Bake in the oven for 15 to 20 minutes until crisp and toasted. Use the oven mitts to remove the muffin pan to the wire rack to cool. Makes 12 toast cups.

GARLIC TOAST CUPS: Stir 1/4 tsp. (1 mL) of garlic powder into the margarine before spreading onto the bread slices.

Bacon & Egg Filler

If you like bacon and eggs, have your breakfast for lunch.

Get It Together: measuring spoons, small bowl, mixing spoon

1. **Large hard-boiled egg, peeled and chopped**	1	1
Bacon slice, cooked crisp and crumbled (or 1 tsp., 5 mL, simulated bacon bits)	1	1
Finely chopped green onion (optional)	2 tsp.	10 mL
Mayonnaise (or salad dressing)	1 tbsp.	15 mL
Salt, sprinkle		
Pepper, sprinkle		
2. **Toast Cups, above**	2	2

1. Combine the first 6 ingredients in the bowl. Stir until moistened.

2. Fill the Toast Cups. Makes 1/3 cup (75 mL).

Crunchy Egg Filling

Try using a pastry blender to chop up the hard-boiled eggs. It works very well. A great filling for sandwiches or Toast Cups, page 118.

Get It Together: dry measures, measuring spoons, small bowl, mixing spoon

1.
Large hard-boiled eggs, peeled and chopped	3	3
Finely chopped cucumber, with peel	1/2 cup	125 mL
Grated carrot	2 tbsp.	30 mL
Thousand Island (or your favourite creamy) dressing	1 1/2-2 tbsp.	25-30 mL
Salt, sprinkle		
Pepper, sprinkle		

1. Combine all 6 ingredients in the bowl. Mix well. Makes 1 1/3 cups (325 mL).

Cream Cheese & Grape Jelly Sandwich

This is very quick and easy to make for lunch.

Get It Together: measuring spoons, table knife, bread knife, cutting board

1.
Spreadable cream cheese	2 tbsp.	30 mL
White (or whole-wheat) bread slices	2	2
Grape jelly	4 tsp.	20 mL

1. Spread the cream cheese on each slice of bread. Spread the jelly on top of the cream cheese on 1 of the slices. Top with the second slice of bread. Cut in half on the cutting board. Makes 1 sandwich.

> **Did you know?**
> Sandwiches made from frozen bread and wrapped immediately in plastic wrap will keep the filling fresh and crisp for hours.

Sliced Turkey Pita

The perfect lunch when you have leftover turkey.

Get It Together: measuring spoons, table knife, dry measures

1. | | | |
   |---|---|---|
   | **Plain spreadable cream cheese** | **3 tbsp.** | **45 mL** |
   | **Pita bread (4 1/2-5 inch,** | **1** | **1** |
   | **11-12.5 cm, size), cut in half** | | |
   | **Cranberry sauce** | **2 tbsp.** | **30 mL** |
   | **Turkey slices** | **4** | **4** |
   | **Alfalfa sprouts (or shredded** | **1/2 cup** | **125 mL** |
   | **lettuce)** | | |

1. Spread the cream cheese on the inner top side of each pita half. Spread the cranberry sauce on the inner bottom side of each pocket. Place 1 slice of turkey in each pocket. Top each slice with the sprouts. Place second slice of turkey over the sprouts. Makes 2 filled pita halves.

Pickly Pita Pockets

A delicious crunch to it. Eat now or make ahead and cover and refrigerate overnight.

Get It Together: dry measures, measuring spoons, small bowl, mixing spoon

1. | | | |
   |---|---|---|
   | **Diced ham (or beef roast** | **1 cup** | **250 mL** |
   | **or salami)** | | |
   | **Finely chopped dill pickles,** | **1/3 cup** | **75 mL** |
   | **blotted dry with paper towel** | | |
   | **Mayonnaise (or salad dressing)** | **2 tbsp.** | **30 mL** |
   | **Prepared mustard** | **1 tsp.** | **5 mL** |
   | **Pita breads (4 1/2-5 inch,** | **2** | **2** |
   | **11-12.5 cm, size), cut in half** | | |

1. Combine the ham, pickles, mayonnaise and mustard in the bowl. Mix well. Fill each pita half with 1/3 cup (75 mL) of the filling. Makes 4 pita halves.

Pictured on page 90.

Veggie Bagel

A messy, but delicious stacked sandwich that's ready in minutes!

Get It Together: toaster, measuring spoons, table knife, bread knife, cutting board

1.	Whole-wheat (or multi-grain) bagel, cut in half	1	1
2.	Plain (or herbed) spreadable cream cheese	1 tbsp.	15 mL
	English cucumber slices, with peel	3-4	3-4
	Tomato slices	1-2	1-2
3.	Salt, sprinkle		
	Pepper, sprinkle		
	Alfalfa sprouts (optional)	1-2 tbsp.	15-30 mL

1. Toast the bagel halves until lightly browned.

2. Spread the cream cheese on both halves. Lay the cucumber and tomato slices on top on 1 half.

3. Sprinkle with salt and pepper. Add the alfalfa sprouts. Top with the second half of the bagel. Cut in half on the cutting board. Makes 1 bagel.

Did you know?
If you are taking a juice box in your lunch, freeze it overnight and pack it in your lunch in the morning. It will keep sandwiches cold and will be thawed by lunchtime.

Tuna Biscuits

Very tasty. Great to take for lunch instead of a sandwich.

Get It Together: muffin pan (for 8 large or 16 mini muffins), dry measures, measuring spoons, medium bowl, whisk, mixing spoon, oven mitts, wire rack

1.			
Large eggs, fork-beaten	2	2
Mayonnaise (or salad dressing)	1/4 cup	60 mL
Tub margarine, melted	2 tbsp.	30 mL
Lemon juice	1/2 tbsp.	7 mL
Hot pepper sauce	1/8 tsp.	0.5 mL

2.			
Cheese-flavoured crackers, coarsely crushed	22	22
Canned solid tuna, drained and flaked	6.5 oz.	184 g
Green onion, sliced	1	1
Finely diced green pepper (optional)	2 tbsp.	30 mL

1. Place the oven rack in the centre position. Turn the oven on to 375°F (190°C). Grease 8 large cups, or 16 mini cups, in the muffin pan. Combine the eggs, mayonnaise, margarine, lemon juice and pepper sauce in the bowl. Beat with the whisk until well blended.

2. Stir the cracker crumbs into the egg mixture. Add the tuna, green onion and green pepper. Stir well to combine. Fill the muffin cups with the mixture. Bake in the oven for 20 minutes for the large cups or for 15 minutes for the mini cups. Use the oven mitts to remove the pan to the wire rack. Makes 8 large biscuits or 16 mini biscuits.

Did you know?

Instead of rushing to make your lunch in the morning before school, try doing as much as possible the night before . . . who knows, you may even have more time to sleep in!

Orange Cranberry Muffins

Using the entire orange gives these muffins lots of vitamins and minerals.

Get It Together: muffin pan (for 12 muffins), sharp knife, blender, liquid measures, dry measures, large bowl, mixing spoon, measuring spoons, wooden toothpick, oven mitts, wire rack

1.

Medium navel orange	1	1
Orange juice	1/2 cup	125 mL
Large egg	1	1
Butter or hard margarine	1/2 cup	125 mL
Dried cranberries (see Note)	1/2 cup	125 mL

2.

All-purpose flour	1 3/4 cups	425 mL
Baking powder	1 tsp.	5 mL
Baking soda	1 tsp.	5 mL
Granulated sugar	2/3 cup	150 mL
Salt	1/2 tsp.	2 mL

1. Place the oven rack in the centre position. Turn the oven on to 400°F (200°C). Grease the muffin pan. Cut the orange into 8 pieces. Place in the blender. Add the orange juice. Process for 1 1/2 minutes or until the orange peel is finely chopped. Add the egg and the butter. Process until blended. Add the dried cranberries and process for 2 seconds.

2. Combine the next 5 ingredients in the large bowl. Mix. Make a well in the centre. Pour the wet ingredients into the well. Stir to moisten. Do not stir too much. Divide the batter between the 12 muffin cups. Bake in the oven for 15 minutes or until golden. The toothpick inserted in the centre of 2 or 3 muffins should come out clean. Use the oven mitts to remove the muffin pan to the wire rack. Let stand for 10 minutes then remove the muffins to the rack to cool completely. Makes 12 muffins.

Note: Frozen cranberries can be substituted for the dried; however, the muffins will be green in colour.

Pictured on page 125.

Apple Granola Muffins

Moist and delicious.

Get It Together: muffin pan (for 12 muffins), medium bowl, dry measures, measuring spoons, mixing spoon, pastry blender, liquid measures, wooden toothpick, oven mitts, wire rack

1.

All-purpose flour	2 cups	500 mL
Baking powder	4 tsp.	20 mL
Salt	1 tsp.	5 mL
Brown sugar, packed	3 tbsp.	45 mL
Ground cinnamon	1/2 tsp.	2 mL

2.

Butter or hard margarine	1/3 cup	75 mL
Apple, cored and chopped	1	1
Milk	1 cup	250 mL
Vanilla flavouring	1 tsp.	5 mL
Granola cereal	1/4 cup	60 mL

1. Place the oven rack in the centre position. Turn the oven on to 400°F (200°C). Grease the muffin pan. Combine the first 5 ingredients in the bowl. Stir well.

2. Add the butter. Cut the butter in with the pastry blender until the flour looks crumbly. Add the apple, milk and vanilla. Stir to moisten. Do not stir too much. Divide the batter between the 12 muffin cups. Sprinkle each with 1 tsp. (5 mL) of granola. Bake in the oven for 20 minutes or until golden. The toothpick inserted in the centre of 2 or 3 muffins should come out clean. Use the oven mitts to remove the muffin pan to the wire rack. Let stand for 10 minutes then remove the muffins to the rack to cool completely. Makes 12 muffins.

Pictured on page 125.

1. Orange Cranberry Muffins, page 123
2. Sesame Honeys, page 132
3. Whole-Wheat Crazy Bread, page 133
4. Apple Granola Muffins, above

Bolts 'N' Things

Lots of different shapes—and flavours—in this. A bit spicy, a bit salty.

Get It Together: dry measures, small saucepan, measuring spoons, mixing spoon, hot pad, large bowl, baking sheet, oven mitts, wire rack, covered container

1.

Tub margarine	1/4 cup	60 mL
Worcestershire sauce	1 tbsp.	15 mL
Seasoning salt	1 tsp.	5 mL
Garlic powder	1/8 tsp.	0.5 mL
Onion powder	1/8 tsp.	0.5 mL

2.

O-shaped toasted oat cereal	2 cups	500 mL
Rice squares cereal	2 cups	500 mL
Mini pretzels	2 cups	500 mL
Cheese squares crackers	2 cups	500 mL
Peanuts	1 cup	250 mL

1. Place the oven rack in the centre position. Turn the oven on to 300°F (150°C). Melt the butter in the saucepan over medium heat. Stir in the next 4 ingredients. Remove the saucepan to the hot pad.

2. Combine the next 5 ingredients in the bowl. Slowly drizzle the butter mixture over the cereal mixture as you keep mixing. Spread on the ungreased baking sheet. Bake in the oven for 15 minutes. Stir well. Bake in the oven for 5 minutes until toasty looking. Use the oven mitts to remove the baking sheet to the wire rack. Cool. Store in the container. You may also freeze this. Makes 9 cups (2.25 L).

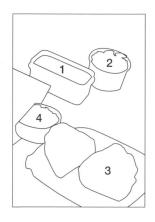

1. Peanut Butter Pudding Dip, page 38
2. Citrus Crunchies, page 128
3. Individual Stuffed Pizzas, page 86
4. Toasted Pumpkin Seeds, page 129

Citrus Crunchies

Great to have on hand for the lunch bag or as a dessert snack.

Get It Together: measuring spoons, microwave-safe cup, microwave oven, dry measures, large bowl, mixing spoon

1. Tub margarine   2 tbsp.   30 mL

2. Rice squares cereal   3 cups   750 mL
   Package lime, orange or   1/2 x 3 oz.   1/2 x 85 g
       grape-flavoured gelatin
       (jelly powder), measure
       3 tbsp., 50 mL

1. Microwave the margarine in the cup on high (100%) for 20 to 30 seconds until melted.

2. Put the cereal into the bowl. Pour the melted margarine over the cereal. Toss until well coated. Sprinkle with the flavoured gelatin. Toss together well. Microwave on high (100%) for 1 minute. Stir. Repeat 3 times. Makes 3 cups (750 mL).

Pictured on page 126.

Fruity Granola

Lots of nutty flavours. But sweetness comes through too.

Get It Together: dry measures, measuring spoons, 2 large bowls, mixing spoon, liquid measures, microwave oven, baking sheet, oven mitts, wire rack

1. Large flake rolled oats   3 cups   750 mL
       (old-fashioned)
   Long thread coconut   1/2 cup   125 mL
   Slivered or sliced almonds   1 cup   250 mL
   Sesame seeds   2 tbsp.   30 mL

2. Tub margarine   1/4 cup   60 mL
   Liquid honey   3 tbsp.   45 mL

3. Chopped dried fruit (such as   2 cups   500 mL
       cherries, apricots, raisins,
       apples or peaches)

(continued on the next page)

128 Snacks

1. Place the oven rack in the centre position. Turn the oven on to 300°F (150°C). Combine the first 4 ingredients in the bowl. Stir.

2. Microwave the margarine and honey in the liquid measure on high (100%) for 1 minute until the margarine is melted and the mixture is bubbling. Pour over the rolled oat mixture and stir well to coat. Spread evenly on the ungreased baking sheet. Bake in the oven for 15 minutes. Stir well and spread the mixture out evenly once more. Bake for 10 minutes until golden brown. Use the oven mitts to remove the baking sheet to the wire rack. Cool.

3. Put the cooled mixture into the other bowl. Stir in the fruit. Makes 7 cups (1.75 L).

Pictured on page 18.

Toasted Pumpkin Seeds

What a treat around Halloween time! Just wash the fresh seeds well and dry them thoroughly on paper towels.

Get It Together: measuring spoons, microwave-safe cup, microwave oven, mixing spoons, dry measures, medium bowl, baking sheet, oven mitts, wire rack

1. **Tub margarine**	**1 tbsp.**	**15 mL**
2. **Seasoning salt**	**1/2 tsp.**	**2 mL**
Paprika	**1/4 tsp.**	**1 mL**
Hot pepper sauce, dash		
3. **Hulled pumpkin seeds (fresh or from the bulk foods or health food store)**	**2 cups**	**500 mL**

1. Place the oven rack in the centre position. Turn the oven on to 250°F (120°C). Microwave the margarine in the cup on high (100%) for 20 to 30 seconds until melted.

2. Stir in the next 3 ingredients.

3. Pour the mixture over the pumpkin seeds in the bowl. Toss well, using 2 spoons, to coat. Spread out on the ungreased baking sheet. Bake in the oven for 10 minutes. Stir. Bake in the oven for 10 minutes until crisp. Use the oven mitts to remove the baking sheet to the wire rack. Cool. Makes 2 cups (500 mL).

Pictured on page 126.

Spicy Corn Corn

Unpopped popcorn will produce larger popped kernels when stored in an airtight container in the refrigerator or freezer.

Get It Together: dry measures, small saucepan, measuring spoons, mixing spoon, hot pad, large paper bag, covered container

1. | | | |
   |---|---|---|
   | Tub margarine | 1/3 cup | 75 mL |
   | Paprika | 1 tsp. | 5 mL |
   | Seasoning salt | 1/2 tsp. | 2 mL |
   | Chili powder | 1/2 tsp. | 2 mL |
   | Cayenne pepper | 1/8 tsp. | 0.5 mL |
   | Liquid smoke (optional), dash | | |

2. | | | |
   |---|---|---|
   | Warm popped popcorn (see Note) | 8 cups | 2 L |
   | Corn chips | 2 cups | 500 mL |
   | Peanuts (or mixed nuts) | 1 cup | 250 mL |
   | Grated Parmesan cheese (or Cheddar cheese powder) | 3 tbsp. | 45 mL |

1. Melt the margarine in the saucepan over medium heat. Add the next 5 ingredients. Stir to combine. Remove the saucepan to the hot pad.

2. Combine the popped popcorn with the corn chips and peanuts in the paper bag. Stir the margarine mixture. Drizzle 1/3 over the popcorn mixture in the bag and add 1 tbsp. (15 mL) of the cheese. Shake the bag well to distribute the margarine and cheese. Repeat 2 times until all of the margarine and cheese are used up. Store any remaining popcorn in the container. Makes 10 cups (2.5 L).

Note: 1/4 cup (60 mL) of unpopped popcorn kernels will make 8 cups of popped corn when made in a hot-air popcorn maker.

Did you know?

Use plastic containers to pack fragile cookies or muffins in your lunch bag. Plastic containers also work best for pickles, dip, salad dressing and other leaky lunch items. For added leakage protection, place a double layer of plastic wrap over the filled container and then put the lid on.

Peanut Butter Popcorn Treats

Just a hint of peanut butter and sweetness.

Get It Together: dry measures, small saucepan, liquid measures, mixing spoon, hot pad, measuring spoons, large bowl, baking sheet, oven mitts, wire rack, covered container

1.	Tub margarine	1/4 cup	60 mL
2.	Brown sugar, packed	1/2 cup	125 mL
	Corn syrup	2/3 cup	150 mL
3.	Smooth peanut butter	1/2 cup	125 mL
	Vanilla flavouring	1 tsp.	5 mL
4.	Popped popcorn	8 cups	2 L

1. Place the oven rack in the centre position. Turn the oven on to 350°F (175°C). Melt the margarine in the saucepan over medium heat.

2. Stir in the sugar and corn syrup. Continue cooking until the sugar is dissolved.

3. Stir in the peanut butter. Bring the mixture to a boil. Remove from the heat to the hot pad. Stir in the vanilla flavouring.

4. Put the popcorn into the bowl. Pour the margarine mixture over the popcorn. Toss well to coat. Spread evenly on the ungreased baking sheet. Bake in the oven for 7 minutes. Use the oven mitts to remove the baking sheet to the wire rack. Cool. Break up the cooled popcorn into bite-size chunks. Store in the container. Makes 8 cups (2 L).

Pictured on page 90.

CHOCO-PEANUT BUTTER POPCORN BALLS: Add 2 tbsp. (30 mL) of cocoa along with the peanut butter to the dissolved sugar mixture in the saucepan. Bring to a boil. Remove from the heat. Add the vanilla flavouring. Pour over the popcorn. Toss well to coat. Cool popcorn mixture long enough so that you can handle it. Grease your hands and make tennis-size balls. Place on waxed paper to let them set. Makes about 14 balls.

Sesame Honeys

These are very tasty. Crisp and chewy.

Get It Together: large bowl, dry measures, measuring spoons, mixing spoon, pastry blender, small bowl, liquid measures, rolling pin, ruler, sharp knife, table fork, cookie sheet, pancake lifter, oven mitts, wire rack, waxed paper

1.	**Whole-wheat flour**	1 cup	250 mL
	All-purpose flour	1 cup	250 mL
	Salt	1 tsp.	5 mL
	Baking powder	1 tsp.	5 mL
	Sesame seeds	1/2 cup	125 mL
2.	**Butter or hard margarine**	1/4 cup	60 mL
3.	**Liquid honey**	1/2 cup	125 mL
	Milk	1/3 cup	75 mL
4.	**Flour**	1-2 tbsp.	15-30 mL

1. Place the oven rack in the centre position. Turn the oven on to 350°F (175°C). Combine the first 5 ingredients in the large bowl. Mix well.

2. Cut in the butter with the pastry blender until crumbly.

3. Stir the honey and milk together in the small bowl. Add to the flour mixture. Stir until it forms a stiff dough.

4. Sprinkle the flour onto the counter or working surface. Use your hands to form the dough into a flat rectangle. Roll to flatten to a 12 x 15 inch (30 x 38 cm) rectangle that is 1/8 to 1/4 inch (3 to 6 mm) thick. Cut into 3 inch (7.5 cm) square crackers with the tip of the sharp knife. Use the pancake lifter to place the crackers on the ungreased cookie sheet. Poke each cracker 3 times with the fork. Bake in the oven for 15 minutes or until golden. Use the oven mitts to remove the cookie sheet to the wire rack. Let stand 2 minutes. Use the pancake lifter to remove the crackers to the waxed paper on the counter. Cool completely. Makes about 20 crackers.

Pictured on page 125.

Whole-Wheat Crazy Bread

This will become a favourite in your home.

Get It Together: 12 inch (30 cm) pizza pan or 10 x 15 inch (25 x 38 cm) baking sheet, 2 small bowls, measuring spoons, dry measures, mixing spoon, medium bowl, liquid measures, whisk, clean cloth, sharp knife, pastry brush, oven mitts, wire rack

1. Fast-rising instant yeast	1 tbsp.	15 mL
Whole-wheat flour	1 cup	250 mL
2. Very warm water	1 cup	250 mL
Cooking oil	1 tbsp.	15 mL
Granulated sugar	1 tsp.	5 mL
Salt	1 tsp.	5 mL
3. All-purpose flour	1 1/2 cups	375 mL
4. Butter or hard margarine, melted	2 tbsp.	30 mL
Garlic powder	1/8 tsp.	0.5 mL
Dried basil	1 tsp.	5 mL
5. Grated Parmesan cheese	2 tbsp.	30 mL

1. Place the oven rack in the centre position. Turn the oven on to 400°F (200°C). Grease the pan. Combine the yeast and whole wheat flour in 1 small bowl. Set aside.

2. Combine the water, cooking oil, sugar and salt in the medium bowl. Stir until dissolved. Add the whole-wheat flour mixture. Whisk until smooth.

3. Add the all-purpose flour. Mix well. Cover the bowl with the cloth. Let stand for 15 minutes.

4. Combine the butter, garlic and basil in the other small bowl. Knead the flour mixture 3 or 4 times. Press out evenly into the greased pan. Cut into 14 sticks or fingers with a sharp knife. Brush the butter mixture over the surface of the dough.

5. Sprinkle with the Parmesan cheese. Cover the baking sheet with the cloth. Let stand 15 minutes. Bake, uncovered, in the oven for 20 minutes or until lightly golden. Use the oven mitts to remove the pan to the wire rack to cool. Makes 14 crazy bread sticks.

Pictured on page 125.

Corn Chowder

Crunchy veggies and thicker creamy base. So quick to make on a cold day.

Get It Together: medium saucepan, mixing spoon, dry measures, measuring spoons, liquid measures, hot pad

1.	Bacon slices, diced	2	2
2.	Chopped onion	1/4 cup	60 mL
	Chopped green or red pepper	1/4 cup	60 mL
	All-purpose flour	1 tbsp.	15 mL
	Milk	1 cup	250 mL
	Canned cream-style corn	14 oz.	398 mL
3.	Parsley flakes	1 tsp.	5 mL
	Hot pepper sauce, dash		
	Pepper, sprinkle		

1. Fry the bacon in the saucepan over medium heat until crisp. Drain off fat.

2. Add the onion and pepper. Cook for 2 minutes until soft. Sprinkle the flour over the vegetables. Stir together well. Slowly stir in the milk and corn. Bring just to a simmer. Remove the saucepan to the hot pad.

3. Add the remaining 3 ingredients. Stir. Makes 3 cups (750 mL).

Pictured on page 108.

Vegetable Chowder

Break up the noodles before you open the package—it's a lot less messy.

Get It Together: measuring spoons, large saucepan, dry measures, mixing spoon, liquid measures

1.	Tub margarine	1 tbsp.	15 mL
	Small onion, chopped	1	1
	Celery rib, chopped	1	1
	Grated carrot	1/4 cup	60 mL
2.	Large potato, with peel, diced	1	1
	Water	5 cups	1.25 L
	Vegetable (or chicken) bouillon powder	1 tbsp.	15 mL

(continued on the next page)

3. Package of instant noodle soup   3 oz.   100 g
       with flavour packet

1. Melt the margarine in the saucepan over medium heat. Add the onion, celery and carrot. Cook, stirring often, until the onion is soft.

2. Stir in the potato, water and bouillon powder. Partially cover, moving the lid slightly to the side to allow a small opening for the steam to escape. Simmer for 15 minutes.

3. Break up the noodles and add, along with the flavour packet, to the simmering mixture in the saucepan. Simmer for 10 minutes. Makes 7 cups (1.75 L).

Hamburger Soup

Double the ingredients and make it for your family. Wholesome and hearty!

Get It Together: medium saucepan, mixing spoon, dry measures, liquid measures, measuring spoons

1.	Lean ground beef	1/2 lb.	225 g
2.	Finely chopped onion	1/4 cup	60 mL
	Finely chopped celery	1/4 cup	60 mL
3.	Medium carrot, cut in half lengthwise, then thinly sliced	1	1
	Medium potato, peeled and diced	1	1
	Water	3 cups	750 mL
	Beef bouillon powder	1 tbsp.	15 mL
4.	Condensed tomato soup	10 oz.	284 mL

1. Scramble-fry the ground beef in the saucepan until no longer pink. Drain off fat.

2. Stir in the onion and celery. Scramble-fry for 3 minutes.

3. Stir in the carrot, potato, water and bouillon powder. Bring to a boil over medium-high heat. Reduce the heat to medium-low. Partially cover, moving the lid slightly to the side to allow a small opening for the steam to escape. Simmer for 20 minutes.

4. Stir in the tomato soup. Heat thoroughly. Makes 5 cups (1.25 L).

Easy Macaroni Soup

Chock full of pasta. Pale orange with bits of green and yellow from the vegetables. This can be warmed up the next day as a creamy mac 'n' cheese (as it will thicken overnight).

Get It Together: liquid measures, measuring spoons, large saucepan, mixing spoon, dry measures, small bowl, whisk

1. | | | |
   |---|---|---|
   | **Water** | **4 cups** | **1 L** |
   | **Seasoning salt** | **1/2 tsp.** | **2 mL** |
   | **Box of macaroni and cheese dinner,** | **7 3/4 oz.** | **225 g** |
   | **cheese flavour packet reserved** | | |

2. | | | |
   |---|---|---|
   | **Frozen mixed vegetables** | **1 cup** | **250 mL** |
   | **Condensed chicken broth** | **10 oz.** | **284 mL** |
   | **Onion powder** | **1 tsp.** | **5 mL** |
   | **Pepper, sprinkle** | | |

3. | | | |
   |---|---|---|
   | **All-purpose flour** | **2 tbsp.** | **30 mL** |
   | **Reserved cheese flavour packet** | | |
   | **Milk** | **1 cup** | **250 mL** |

1. Bring the water and seasoning salt to a boil in the saucepan. Add the macaroni only from the package. Boil for 5 minutes, stirring occasionally.

2. Add the vegetables, chicken broth, onion powder and pepper. Return to a boil and cook for 5 minutes.

3. Combine the flour and cheese flavour packet in the bowl. Slowly add the milk, whisking it until smooth. Add to the macaroni and vegetables in the saucepan. Cook, stirring constantly, for 2 or 3 minutes. Makes 7 cups (1.75 L).

Pictured on page 36.

Colour-Full Bean Soup

Tasty balance of flavours between the ham and the beans. Name says it all.

Get It Together: measuring spoons, large saucepan, dry measures, mixing spoon, liquid measures

1. | | | |
   |---|---|---|
   | Tub margarine | 1 tbsp. | 15 mL |
   | Chopped onion | 1/2 cup | 125 mL |
   | Chopped celery | 1/2 cup | 125 mL |

2. | | | |
   |---|---|---|
   | Medium carrot, grated | 1 | 1 |
   | Water | 2 cups | 500 mL |
   | Medium potato, peeled and diced | 1 | 1 |
   | Canned mixed beans, with liquid | 19 oz. | 540 mL |
   | Bay leaf | 1 | 1 |
   | Chili powder | 1/2 tsp. | 2 mL |
   | Parsley flakes | 1/2 tsp. | 2 mL |
   | Pepper | 1/8 tsp. | 0.5 mL |

3. | | | |
   |---|---|---|
   | Canned flaked ham, crumbled (or 1/2 cup, 125 mL, finely chopped cooked ham) | 6 1/2 oz. | 184 g |

1. Melt the margarine in the saucepan over medium heat. Cook the onion and celery, stirring often, until soft.

2. Add the next 8 ingredients. Bring to a boil. Reduce the heat to low. Cover. Simmer for 20 minutes.

3. Add the ham. Stir. Cover and simmer for 5 minutes. Makes 6 cups (1.5 L).

Did you know?

Whenever you're cooking something on the stove, it's wise to fit your pan size to the burner size—don't put a small pan on a great big burner! For safety, turn pan handles so they don't stick out over the edge of the stove, but make sure they're not over another burner.

Bean 'N' Bacon Soup

Make this as zippy as you want with the hot pepper sauce. This is a chunky soup with lots of liquid.

Get It Together: large saucepan, mixing spoon, liquid measures, measuring spoons

1. Bacon slices, diced	2	2
Small onion, chopped	1	1
2. Large potato, peeled and diced	1	1
Water	2 cups	500 mL
3. Condensed vegetable soup	10 oz.	284 mL
Canned beans in tomato sauce, mashed with a fork	14 oz.	398 mL
Hot pepper sauce	1/8-1/4 tsp.	0.5-1 mL
4. Grated Cheddar cheese, sprinkle (for garnish)		

1. Fry the bacon in the saucepan over medium heat for 2 minutes. Add the onion. Cook for about 5 minutes, stirring often, until the bacon is cooked and the onion is soft.

2. Add the potato and water. Cover and bring to a boil over medium heat for 10 to 12 minutes until the potato is tender.

3. Stir in the vegetable soup, beans and pepper sauce. Simmer, uncovered, for 10 minutes.

4. Garnish with Cheddar cheese. Makes 5 1/2 cups (1.4 L).

Pictured on page 144.

Variation: Substitute condensed cream of celery soup or condensed cream of mushroom soup for the vegetable soup.

> ### Did you know?
> To keep soups nice and warm until lunch, preheat your thermos at the last possible moment before filling it. First, fill the thermos with boiling water and let stand for 5 minutes. Pour out the hot water. Fill the thermos with the hot soup. Seal it tightly.

Corn Doggies

Make these the night before and simply reheat for lunch. These also freeze well.

Get It Together: medium bowl, dry measures, measuring spoons, table fork, rolling pin, ruler, table knife, pastry brush, baking sheet, oven mitts, wire rack

1.

Envelope of pie crust mix	1 x 9 1/2 oz.	1 x 270 g
Cornmeal	1/3 cup	75 mL
Chili powder	1 tsp.	5 mL
Cold water, approximately	6 tbsp.	100 mL
All-purpose flour, as needed, to prevent sticking when rolling		

2.

Wieners	8	8
Large egg, fork-beaten	1	1

1. Place the oven rack in the centre position. Turn the oven on to 450°F (230°F). Pour the pie crust mix into the bowl. Stir in the cornmeal and chili powder. Slowly add the cold water, 1 tbsp. (15 mL) at a time, stirring with a fork after each addition. The dough should start to pull away from the sides of the bowl and form a ball. Divide in half. Roll each half into a 5 x 12 inch (12.5 x 30 cm) rectangle on a lightly floured counter or working surface. Cut each rectangle crosswise into 4 equal rectangles.

2. Place a wiener lengthwise across each rectangle. Brush 1 of the long edges of the pastry with the egg. Bring the 2 long edges of the rectangle up over the wiener and press together to seal. Place seam side down on the ungreased baking sheet. Repeat with each rectangle. Brush each surface with remaining egg. Bake in the oven for 12 minutes until crisp and golden. Use the oven mitts to remove the baking sheet to the wire rack. Makes 8 wrapped wieners.

Pictured on page 144.

Vegetable Roll

Try different flavoured dressings for a variety of tastes.

Get It Together: measuring spoons, small bowl, mixing spoon, table knife, dry measures, plastic wrap

1.	Spreadable cream cheese	1 tbsp.	15 mL
	Ranch (or other creamy) dressing	1 tbsp.	15 mL
	White (or whole-wheat) flour tortilla (10 inch, 25 cm, size)	1	1
2.	Grated carrot	2 tbsp.	30 mL
	Finely chopped green, red or yellow pepper	2 tbsp.	30 mL
	Finely chopped green onion	2 tsp.	10 mL
	Finely chopped broccoli florets	3 tbsp.	45 mL
	Grated Cheddar cheese	1/4 cup	60 mL

1. Combine the cream cheese and dressing in the bowl. Stir. Spread the cream cheese mixture on the tortilla, almost to the edge.

2. Sprinkle with the remaining 5 ingredients in the order given. Roll up tightly and wrap with plastic wrap. Chill in the refrigerator. Makes 1 roll.

Pictured on page 35.

Did you know?
Flour tortillas keep well in a sealed plastic bag in the refrigerator for up to 2 weeks. They can even be frozen. Be creative and use flour tortillas the next time you reach for the bread slices.

"Wurst" Cheese & Lettuce Wrap

Very easy and quick to make. Spread as much liverwurst on the tortilla as you like.

Get It Together: measuring spoons, table knife, dry measures, plastic wrap

1.			
Plain (or herbed) liverwurst	2-3 tbsp.	30-45 mL
White (or whole-wheat) flour tortilla (10 inch, 25 cm, size)	1	1
Grated Swiss cheese	1/3 cup	75 mL
Shredded lettuce	1/3-1/2 cup	75-125 mL

1. Spread the liverwurst on the tortilla. Sprinkle with the cheese and lettuce. Roll up tightly and wrap with plastic wrap. Chill in the refrigerator. Makes 1 wrap.

Pictured on page 143.

Roast Beef Roll

Try this dipped in Honey Mustard Dunk, page 32.

Get It Together: measuring spoons, table knife, dry measures, plastic wrap

1.			
Plain (or herbed) spreadable cream cheese	3 tbsp.	45 mL
White (or whole-wheat) flour tortilla (10 inch, 25 cm, size)	1	1
Shredded lettuce	1/2 cup	125 mL
Finely diced onion	1 tbsp.	15 mL
Shaved roast beef (or 3 very thin slices)	2 oz.	57 g

1. Spread the cream cheese on 1 side of the tortilla. Cover with the lettuce and onion. Lay the beef over top. Roll up tightly and wrap with plastic wrap. Chill in the refrigerator for at least 1 hour or overnight. Makes 1 roll.

Pictured on page 143.

Lettuce Rolls

These are best made in the morning before school. Lettuce leaves will become soggy if rolls are made the night before. Peel down the plastic wrap as you eat the roll.

Get It Together: measuring spoons, table knife, plastic wrap

1.			
Large lettuce leaves		4	4
Ham slices (or other sliced deli meat)		2	2
Prepared mustard (or mayonnaise)		1 tbsp.	15 mL

1. Lay lettuce leaves on the working surface, making 2 stacks of 2 lettuce leaves each. Lay 1 slice of ham over each lettuce stack. Spread mustard over the ham. Roll up tightly and wrap with plastic wrap. Chill in the refrigerator. Makes 2 rolls.

Variation: Place a carrot stick, cheese stick, dill pickle wedge or folded cheese slice on the top of the ham before rolling.

1. Pizza Sticks (with Dipping Sauce), page 92
2. Smoked Salmon Spread, page 40
3. Jam & Cheese Spread, page 34
4. "Wurst" Cheese & Lettuce Wrap, page 141
5. Roast Beef Rolls, page 141

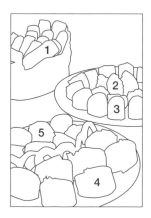

Ham & Cheese Delights

Take one or two of these for your school lunch. Great warm or cold.

Get It Together: measuring spoons, medium bowl, mixing spoon, table knife, baking sheet, oven mitts, wire rack

1.		
Cream cheese, softened	8 oz.	250 g
Sweet pickle relish	1 1/2 tbsp.	25 mL
Ham slices, diced	5	5
Onion powder	1/4 tsp.	1 mL
2.		
Tube of refrigerator crescent rolls (8 rolls per tube)	8 1/2 oz.	235 g

1. Place the oven rack in the centre position. Turn the oven on to 375°F (190°C). Combine the cream cheese, relish, ham and onion powder in the bowl. Mix well.

2. Open the crescent roll tube and separate the rolls into 8 triangles. Spread 2 tbsp. (30 mL) of the ham mixture on each triangle. Roll from the shortest side of the triangle to the opposite point. Place the rolls on the ungreased baking sheet. Bake in the oven for 12 minutes until golden brown. Use the oven mitts to remove the baking sheet to the wire rack. Makes 8 "delights."

Pictured on page 18.

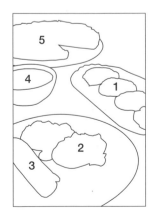

1. Ham Stacks, page 75
2. Broccoli-Sauced Potatoes, page 66
3. Corn Doggies, page 139
4. Bean 'N' Bacon Soup (variation), page 138
5. Pass-Da Pizza, page 81

Cucumber Under Wraps

Pack these for your lunch. Easy to eat.

Get It Together: measuring spoons, table knife, plastic wrap

1.	**Plain (or herbed) spreadable cream cheese**	1/2 cup	125 mL
	White (or whole-wheat) flour tortillas (10 inch, 25 cm, size)	4	4
2.	**English cucumber piece, 8 inches (20 cm) long, quartered lengthwise**	1	1
	Salt, sprinkle (optional)		
	Pepper, sprinkle (optional)		

1. Spread 2 tbsp. (30 mL) of the cream cheese on each tortilla.

2. Lay 1 cucumber spear across 1 side of each tortilla. Sprinkle with salt and pepper. Roll each tortilla around the cucumber. Wrap tightly with plastic wrap. Chill in the refrigerator. Makes 4 wraps.

Peanut Butter Wrap

Much more fun than your ordinary peanut butter sandwich.

Get It Together: measuring spoons, table knife, dry measures, small cup, small spoon, plastic wrap

1.	**Peanut butter**	2 tbsp.	30 mL
	White (or whole-wheat) flour tortilla (10 inch, 25 cm, size)	1	1
	Chopped apple, with peel	1/2 cup	125 mL
2.	**Brown sugar, packed**	1 tsp.	5 mL
	Ground cinnamon	1/4 tsp.	1 mL

1. Spread the peanut butter on the tortilla. Scatter the apple over the top.

2. Combine the sugar and cinnamon in the cup. Sprinkle over the apple. Roll tortilla up tightly and wrap with plastic wrap. Chill in the refrigerator. Makes 1 wrap.

Mexican Stir-Fry Wraps

Lots of colour! Great taste! Change the spiciness according to your preference.

Get It Together: measuring spoons, frying pan, mixing spoon,
dry measures, hot pad

1. Cooking oil | 1 tsp. | 5 mL
   Boneless, skinless chicken breast | 1 | 1
   half (about 4 oz., 113 g), slivered

2. Garlic powder | 1/8 tsp. | 0.5 mL
   Salt | 1/8 tsp. | 0.5 mL
   Pepper, sprinkle

3. Small red (or other mild) | 1/2 | 1/2
   onion, thinly sliced
   Medium green, red or yellow | 1/2 | 1/2
   pepper, slivered
   Salsa | 1/3 cup | 75 mL

4. White (or whole-wheat) flour | 3 | 3
   tortillas (10 inch, 25 cm, size)

1. Heat the cooking oil in the frying pan over medium-high heat. Stir-fry the chicken for 2 minutes.

2. Add the garlic powder, salt and pepper. Cook for 2 minutes.

3. Add the onion and green pepper to the chicken. Stir-fry for 3 minutes. Add the salsa and stir-fry for 2 minutes until the vegetables are tender-crisp. Remove the frying pan to the hot pad. Makes 2 cups (500 mL).

4. Divide the mixture evenly among the 3 tortillas. Fold, envelope-style, by bringing the bottom edge of the tortilla to the centre, over the chicken mixture. Fold the left side over the centre and then fold the right side over the centre, overlapping the left side. Makes 3 smaller tortilla wraps.

Pictured on page 72.

Measurement Tables

Throughout this book measurements are given in Conventional and Metric measure. To compensate for differences between the two measurements due to rounding, a full metric measure is not always used. The cup used is the standard 8 fluid ounce. Temperature is given in degrees Fahrenheit and Celsius. Baking pan measurements are in inches and centimetres as well as quarts and litres. An exact metric conversion is given below as well as the working equivalent (Metric Standard Measure).

Spoons

Conventional Measure	Metric Exact Conversion Millilitre (mL)	Metric Standard Measure Millilitre (mL)
1/8 teaspoon (tsp.)	0.6 mL	0.5 mL
1/4 teaspoon (tsp.)	1.2 mL	1 mL
1/2 teaspoon (tsp.)	2.4 mL	2 mL
1 teaspoon (tsp.)	4.7 mL	5 mL
2 teaspoons (tsp.)	9.4 mL	10 mL
1 tablespoon (tbsp.)	14.2 mL	15 mL

Cups

Conventional Measure	Metric Exact Conversion Millilitre (mL)	Metric Standard Measure Millilitre (mL)
1/4 cup (4 tbsp.)	56.8 mL	60 mL
1/3 cup (5 1/3 tbsp.)	75.6 mL	75 mL
1/2 cup (8 tbsp.)	113.7 mL	125 mL
2/3 cup (10 2/3 tbsp.)	151.2 mL	150 mL
3/4 cup (12 tbsp.)	170.5 mL	175 mL
1 cup (16 tbsp.)	227.3 mL	250 mL
4 1/2 cups	1022.9 mL	1000 mL (1 L)

Oven Temperatures

Fahrenheit (°F)	Celsius (°C)
175°	80°
200°	95°
225°	110°
250°	120°
275°	140°
300°	150°
325°	160°
350°	175°
375°	190°
400°	200°
425°	220°
450°	230°
475°	240°
500°	260°

Dry Measurements

Conventional Measure Ounces (oz.)	Metric Exact Conversion Grams (g)	Metric Standard Measure Grams (g)
1 oz.	28.3 g	28 g
2 oz.	56.7 g	57 g
3 oz.	85.0 g	85 g
4 oz.	113.4 g	125 g
5 oz.	141.7 g	140 g
6 oz.	170.1 g	170 g
7 oz.	198.4 g	200 g
8 oz.	226.8 g	250 g
16 oz.	453.6 g	500 g
32 oz.	907.2 g	1000 g (1 kg)

Pans

Conventional Inches	Metric Centimetres
8x8 inch	20x20 cm
9x9 inch	23x23 cm
9x13 inch	23x33 cm
10x15 inch	25x38 cm
11x17 inch	28x43 cm
8x2 inch round	20x5 cm
9x2 inch round	23x5 cm
10x4 1/2 inch tube	25x11 cm
8x4x3 inch loaf	20x10x7.5 cm
9x5x3 inch loaf	23x12.5x7.5 cm

Casseroles

CANADA & BRITAIN		UNITED STATES	
Standard Size Casserole	Exact Metric Measure	Standard Size Casserole	Exact Metric Measure
1 qt. (5 cups)	1.13 L	1 qt. (4 cups)	900 mL
1 1/2 qts. (7 1/2 cups)	1.69 L	1 1/2 qts. (6 cups)	1.35 L
2 qts. (10 cups)	2.25 L	2 qts. (8 cups)	1.8 L
2 1/2 qts. (12 1/2 cups)	2.81 L	2 1/2 qts. (10 cups)	2.25 L
3 qts. (15 cups)	3.38 L	3 qts. (12 cups)	2.7 L
4 qts. (20 cups)	4.5 L	4 qts. (16 cups)	3.6 L
5 qts. (25 cups)	5.63 L	5 qts. (20 cups)	4.5 L

Recipe Index

C

152   Recipe Index

156   Recipe Index

V

W

Y

HEALTHY COOKING SERIES

To your health—and bon appétit!

You've asked and Company's Coming has listened! The new Healthy Cooking Series delivers delicious healthy recipes and nutrition information from leading health and wellness experts. These beautiful, full-colour cookbooks will transform the way you eat—and the way you live!

Now Available!

Now Available!

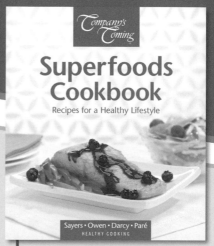

Finally—a book that shows you how to make delicious baked goods and sweets that are completely gluten-free. Ted Wolff, founder of Kinnikinnick Foods, makes living gluten-free easy in this highly requested title.

Blueberries lower your risk for cardiovascular disease, and walnuts reduce your risk of diabetes and cancer. With these recipes, you can easily add superfoods to your daily diet and improve your health and well-being.

Visit our website for sample recipes and more information:

www.companyscoming.com

Canadian Culinary
Olympic Chefs
Cook at Home

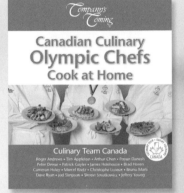

Only the country's best chefs have what it takes to represent Canada at the World Culinary Olympics, and in this book they share their favourite recipes, the ones they cook at home for their families.

These are gourmet recipes for real people, easy enough to make at home using everyday ingredients.

CANADA COOKS SERIES

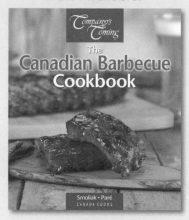
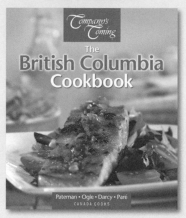
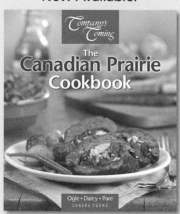
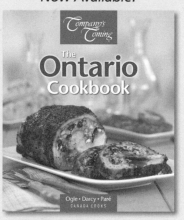